# THE INDUSTRIES OF ANIMALS

# THE INDUSTRIES OF ANIMALS

By

**FRÉDÉRIC HOUSSA Y.**

**WITH 44 ILLUSTRATIONS**

GYAN

*Published by*

GYAN

Gyan Publishing House
5, Ansari Road
Daryaganj, New Delhi-110002
Phone: 011-47034999, 9811692060
E-mail: books@gyanbooks.com

*Distribution Network*
gyanbooks.com
India, USA, Canada, UK, Australia, France



ISBN : 978-81-212-6577-5 (PB)
First Published, 1893

2nd Impression 2022

*Printed at:* Gyan Press, Delhi.



**THE INDUSTRIES OF ANIMALS**
Author: FRÉDÉRIC HOUSSA Y.

# THE INDUSTRIES OF ANIMALS.

BY

FRÉDÉRIC HOUSSAY.

WITH 44 ILLUSTRATIONS.

1893.

## NOTE.

The English edition of this book has been revised throughout and enlarged, with the author's co-operation. Numerous bibliographical references have also been added. The illustrations, when not otherwise stated, are in most cases adapted from Brehm's *Thierleben.*

# CONTENTS.

## CHAPTER I.



## CHAPTER II.



## CHAPTER III.

# THE INDUSTRIES OF ANIMALS.

# THE INDUSTRIES OF ANIMALS.

## CHAPTER I.

### INTRODUCTION.

THE NATURALISTS OF YESTERDAY AND THE NATURALISTS OF TO-DAY—NATURAL HISTORY AND THE NATURAL SCIENCES—THE THEORY OF EVOLUTION—THE CHIEF INDUSTRIES OF MAN—THE CHIEF INDUSTRIES OF ANIMALS—INTELLIGENCE AND INSTINCT—INSTINCTIVE ACTIONS ORIGINATE IN REFLECTIVE ACTIONS—THE PLAN OF STUDY OF THE VARIOUS INDUSTRIES.

*The naturalists of yesterday and the naturalists of to-day.*—The study of animals, plants, rocks, and of natural objects generally, was formerly called "natural history"; but this term is tending to disappear from our vdoabulary and to give place to the term "natural sciences." What is the reason of this change, and to what does it correspond? for it is rare for a word to be modified in so short a time if the thing designated has not itself varied.

Exterior forms have certainly changed, and the naturalist of yesterday makes upon us the impression of a legendary being. I refer to the person described in George Sand's romances, marching vigorously over hills and valleys in search of a rare insect, which he pricked with delight, or of a plant difficult to reach, which he triumphantly dried and fixed on a leaf of paper bearing the date of the discovery and the name of the locality. A herbarium became a sort of journal, recalling to its fortunate possessor all the wanderings of the happy chase, all the delightful sounds and sights of the country. Every naturalist concealed within him a lover of idylls or eclogues. Assuredly all the preliminary studies which resulted from these excursions were necessary; we owe gratitude to our predecessors, and we profit from their labours, sometimes regretting the loss of the picturesque fashion in which their researches were carried out.

The naturalist of to-day usually lives more in the laboratory than in the country. Occasional expeditions to the coast or dredgings are the only links that attach him to nature; the scalpel and the microtome have replaced the collector's pins, and the magnifying glass gives place to the microscope. When the observer begins to pursue his studies in the laboratory he no longer cares to pass the threshold. He has still so much to learn concerning the most common creatures that it seems useless to him to waste his time in seeking those that are rarer, unless he takes into account the unquestionable pleasure of rambling through woods or along coasts;—but such a consideration does not belong to the scientific domain.

A change of conditions of this nature does not suffice to create a science. To take away from a study all that rendered it pleasant and easy, and to make it the property of a small coterie, when it was formerly accessible to all, is not sufficient to render it scientific. It is a fatality rather than a triumph to have undergone such a change. The change is an effect rather than a cause.

When little or nothing was known it was necessary to begin by examining the phenomena which first met the eyes of the observer, such as the customs of animals and the characters which distinguished them from each other. Their differences and resemblances were studied; they were formed into groups, classed and arranged in an order recalling as much as possible their natural relations. In classifying it is impossible to consider all the facts or the result would be chaos; it is necessary to choose the characters and to give preponderance to certain of them. This sorting of characters has been executed with the sagacity of genius by the illustrious naturalists of the last century and the beginning of the present. But the frames which they have traced are fixed and rigid; nature with her infinite plasticity escapes from them. We render a great homage to the classifiers when we say that they have confined the facts as closely as it is possible to do. The catalogues which they have prepared are of a utility which is unquestionable, although their *rôle* is to be useful only; we cannot pretend to make them the expression, the symbol, the formula in which all natural phenomena are to be enclosed. To confound classification with science is to confound the lever with the effect which we expect from it.

Curiosity, moreover, always impels towards that which is least known. External appearances having been studied, the form and function of internal organs were investigated. Physiology and comparative anatomy were born and developed; researches abounded and observers abandoned the field for the laboratory.

The difference in methods of research and the pushing of precision to its extreme limits—an inevitable result of the different nature of the observations to be made—did not however yet render legitimate the claim for natural studies to be called "science."

*Natural history and the natural sciences.*—A more important event has taken place. The ancient naturalists, like their contemporaries, had firm beliefs which they used as unquestionable principles for the comprehension of all facts. The explanation of an observation was ready in advance. The study of facts invariably brought to the pen of the writer the same enthusiastic admiration of the marvellous part played by Providence in nature.[1] The phenomena in which this action was not strikingly apparent were merely described without any attempt to relate them with each other, or with the other facts. A hypothesis which left a great number of facts without explanation was necessarily insufficient. The descriptions, in spite of all their individual interest, did not constitute a homogeneous whole, a science. They were merely a collection of more or less natural histories.

Science only begins on the day when we have found the simple theory which binds together all the facts at that time known, without of course prejudicing the future. As the number of acquired facts increases, if the theory in question continues to explain the new as it explained the old, the science

[1] See, for example, Réaumur, *Mémoires pour l'histoire des Insectes*, t. i., pp. 23-25.

becomes more firmly established. If we can imagine a time arriving when all the possible phenomena are known, and the existing hypothesis still explains them, nothing henceforth can overturn it, the science is completed. That is the simple case in which a theory has been victorious; but if it is contradicted by a single well-authenticated fact it must fall or become modified. The more things a theory explains in the present the more chance it has of success in the future. It is still only a matter of chances, for the theory is always at the mercy of unforeseen observation, which may rudely overthrow it.

There is no theory which must not be modified constantly, at least in its details. To render it more and more general by successive improvements is the aim to be pursued. A collection of studies constitutes a science when a hypothesis has arisen already sufficiently strong to oblige us to refer to it all new acquisitions, and to compel us to see if they fortify or oppose it.

It would indeed be a narrow conception if we were to consider as scientific the partisans of the theory alone; more than anywhere else discussion is fruitful in the natural sciences; and if it is necessary to be constantly preoccupied with the general ideas of the day, it is not at all necessary to adhere to them servilely. The naturalists of to-day are in possession of a formula with which we must always preoccupy ourselves; in other words, there are natural sciences.

*The theory of Evolution.*—This hypothesis which comes before all others is the theory of evolution. This is not the place to expound it, to go over the proofs which have been amassed to build it up, nor the criticisms which have been directed against it. It has to-day come out of the struggle victoriously. A prodigious quantity of facts, of comparative anatomy and of embryology, inexplicable without it, emerge from the chaos and constitute a whole, truly and marvellously homogeneous. Issued from the natural sciences, the doctrine of evolution now overflows them and tends to embrace everything that concerns man: history, sociology, political economy, psychology. The moralists seek, and will surely find, compromises permitting ethical laws to endure the rule of this overwhelming hypothesis.

Without going too far back into history, let us look towards the end of the last century and the beginning of this. Cuvier, Lamarck,[1] and Geoffroy Saint-Hilaire,[2] all preoccupied with general ideas, were each trying to build up a doctrine. The theory of evolution was born beneath the pen of Lamarck, but immediately fell under the attacks of Cuvier.[3] It is to Darwin that the honour belongs of having rescued it from oblivion and of having initiated the movement which to-day rules the natural sciences. Studies in embryology and anatomy are rising without number beneath this impulse; and perhaps it may be said that these new sciences, so fruitful in results, absorb a little too much attention and leave in the shade subjects longer known, but which, however, gain new interest by the way they fit into present scientific theories.

I wish to speak of the manners of animals; the

[1] *Philosophie zoologique*, 2e édition, Paris, 1830; *Histoire des Animaux sans Vertèbres*, Introduction, 1835.

[2] *Philosophie anatomique*, 1818; *Zoologie générale*, 1841.

[3] *Le Règne Animal*, 1829; *Leçons d'Anatomie comparée*, 2e édition, 1835-46.

facts regarding them are of sufficient interest if we consider them one by one, and they become much more interesting when we attempt to show the close way in which they are bound together. Volumes would not suffice to exhaust the subject; but if the entire task is too considerable, I may at least hope to accomplish a part of it by treating of those facts which may be brought together under the common title of Animal Industries. Taken separately, they may be reproached with a certain anecdotal character, but we cannot fail to agree that taken altogether they constitute an important chapter in the sciences of life.

*The chief industries of Man.*—Let us first throw a rapid glance at the various stages which the civilisation and industry of Man have gone through before arriving at their present condition. To make clear these phases we might either follow the state of civilisation in any given country by tracing back the course of centuries, or else at a given epoch find out in different parts of the earth all the stages of human evolution. The savage men of to-day are not further advanced in their evolution than our own ancestors who have now gone to fossil. However it may be, Man, at first frugivorous, as his dentition shows as well as his zoological affinities, in consequence of a famine of fruit or from whatever other cause, gradually began to nourish himself with the flesh of other animals. To search for this fleeing prey developed in him the art of hunting and fishing. His intelligence, still feeble, was entirely concentrated on this one point: to seize on an animal and to feed on it, although neither his nails nor his teeth nor his muscles make it natural to him. To hunt, to fish, to defend his territory against the wild beasts who attacked it and himself, to drive back tribes of his fellows who would diminish his provisions, these were the first rudiments of the industry of Man. Having become more skilful, he obtained in an expedition more game than he could consume at once; he then kept near him living beasts in order to sacrifice them when hunger came. His reserve of animals increased; they became accustomed to live near him; and he took care of his larder. A flock was gradually constituted, and the owner learnt to profit from all the resources which it offered him, from milk to wool. Henceforth he became economical with his beasts, and moved about in order to procure for them abundance of grass and water. He was still always hunting and fighting; but there were now accessory industries, and he was especially occupied in the domestication of animals. Then it happened that he acquired a taste for a graminaceous grain—corn. To seek the blades one by one is not a very fruitful labour, and decidedly troublesome. Man collected a supply of them, cultivated them, possessed fields which he sowed and harvested. He was henceforth obliged to renounce his herds, which had become immense; for he could not leave the soil where his corn was ripening, if he wished to gather it himself, and his cattle were lacking pasture. The number of beasts diminished; bread had killed milk. Man only kept near him a small flock capable of feeding on a moderate territory. He abandoned his temporary shelters, tents of skin or of woven wool, and since he must henceforth live on the same piece of land, he constructed there a fixed dwelling. Such is, taken altogether, the genesis of the industry of the dwelling connected with the culture of the soil; to earlier periods corresponded the natural or hollowed cave and the woven tent.

*The chief industries of Animals.*—In a more or less perfect degree we find the same industries among animals generally. In order to make just comparisons, we ought especially to consider the methods of those who are not endowed with specially appropriated organs, for in this case their task is rendered too simple. To take an example. The Lion is certainly an incomparable hunter; but his whole organisation tends to facilitate the capture of living prey. His agility and the strength of his muscles enable him to seize it at the first leap before it can escape. With his sharp claws he holds it; his teeth are so keen and his jaw so strong that he kills it immediately; with such natural advantages what need has he of ingenuity? But in the case of the Wolf or the Fox it is quite another matter; they hunt with a veritable art which Man himself has not disdained, since he has taken as his associate their relative, the Dog. It is the same with the Eagle and the Crow. The latter, in order to seize the prey which he desires, needs much more varied resources than the great bird of rapine for whom nature has done everything.

We find among animals not only hunting and fishing but the art of storing in barns, of domesticating various species, of harvesting and reaping—the rudiments of the chief human industries. Certain animals in order to shelter themselves take advantage of natural caverns in the same way as many races of primitive men. Others, like the Fox and the Rodents, dig out dwellings in the earth; even to-day there are regions where Man does not act otherwise, preparing himself a lodging by excavations in the chalk or the tufa. Woven dwellings, constructed with materials entangled in one another, like the nests of birds, proceed from the same method of manufacture as the woollen stuffs of which nomad tribes make their tents. The Termites who construct vast dwellings of clay, the Beavers who build huts of wood and of mud, have in this industry reached the same point as Man. They do not build so well, no doubt, nor in so complex a fashion as modern architects and engineers, but they work in the same way. All these ingenious artisans operate without organs specially adapted to accomplish the effect which they reach. It is with such genuine industries that we have to deal, for the most part neglecting other productions, more marvellous in certain ways, which are formed by particular organs, or are elaborated within the organism, and are not the result of the intelligent effort of the individual. To this category belong the threads which the Spider stretches, and the cocoon with which the Caterpillar surrounds himself to shelter his metamorphosis.

*Intelligence and instinct.*—By attentive observation it is possible to find in animals all the intermediate stages between a deliberate reflective action and an act that has become instinctive and so inveterate to the species that it has re-acted on its body, and thus profoundly modified it so as to produce a new organ in such a way that the phenomena are accomplished as a simple function of vegetative life, in the same way as respiration or digestion.

If an individual is led to reproduce often the same

series of actions it contracts a *habit;* the repetition may be so frequent that the animal comes to accomplish it without knowing it; the brain no longer intervenes; the spinal cord or the chain of ganglia alone govern this order of acts, to which has been given the name of *reflex actions.* A reflex may be so powerful as to be transmitted by heredity to the descendants; it then becomes an *instinct.*

Thus by its nature instinct does not differ from intelligence, but is intimately connected with it by a chain of which all the links may be counted. The most intelligent of beings, Man, performs actions that are purely mechanical; many indeed can with justice be called instinctive; and, on the other hand, an animal for whom an innate hereditary instinct is sufficient in ordinary life will give proof of intelligence and reflection if circumstances in which his instinct is generally efficacious become modified so that he can no longer profit by them. Among other ingenious experiments to show the supposed difference between instinctive and reflective acts, Fabre brings forward the following[1]:—The *Chalicodoma*, a hymenopterous relative of the Bees, constructs nests composed of cells formed of mud agglutinated with saliva. The cell once constructed, the insect begins to fill it with honey before laying an egg there. He returns with his booty and wishes to disburse himself in the nest, finds the cellule which he has to fill, and proceeds always in the same order: first, he plunges his head in the cell and disgorges the honey which fills his crop; secondly, he emerges from the cell, turns round, and lets fall the pollen which remains attached to his legs. Suppose

[1] J. H. Fabre, *Souvenirs entomologiques,* Paris, 1879, pp. 275 *et seq.*

that an insect has just disgorged his honey, the observer touches his belly with a straw; the little animal, disturbed in his operation, returns to it having only the second act to perform. But he re-commences the whole of his operations though having nothing more to disgorge ; he again plunges his head into the cell and goes through a pretence of disgorging, then turns round and frees himself from the pollen. Although touched twice, thrice, or more frequently, he always repeats the first action before executing the second. It is, says Fabre, almost like the movement of a machine of which the wheelwork will not act until one has begun to turn the wheel which directs it.

It is incontestable ; but I would add, as this conscientious observer does not, that that does not prove that the intelligence of the insect differs essentially from ours ; it is a simple question of degree. Look at a boy who is going to jump over a ditch : he begins by spitting into his hands and rubbing them one against the other before taking his spring. In what has this served him? It is not more intelligent than the gesture of the bee who first plunges his head in the cell before freeing his claws, although the first gesture is useless.[1]

And, from another side, if nothing is more instinctive than the manner in which domestic Bees construct their cells of wax with geometric regularity, there are other circumstances in which these same

[1] It should perhaps be added that while the boy's action is not consciously intelligent, it is by no means purposeless, and is therefore not quite parallel with the insect's. By vigorously irritating the sensory nerves of the hand the boy imparts a stimulus to his muscular system. His act belongs to a large group which has been especially studied by Féré. See his *Sensation et Mouvement* (1887), and *Pathologie des Emotions* (1892).

insects give proof of remarkable reflection, sagacity, and intelligence in co-ordinating their actions in the presence of an event to which they are not accustomed, and in attaining an end which has presented itself by accident. Such are, for example, the arrangements which they make to defend their honey against the attacks of a great nocturnal Moth, the Death's Head. I shall have to revert to these facts.

We must not then regard instinct, as has often been done, as a rudiment of intelligence, susceptible or not of development; but much rather as a series of intelligent acts at first reasoned, then by their frequent repetition become habitual, reflex, and at last, by heredity, instinctive.

What the individual loses in individuality and in personal initiative, heredity restores to him in the form of instinct which is, as it were, the condensed and accumulated intelligence of his ancestors. He himself no longer needs to take thought either to preserve his life or to assure the perpetuation of his race. The qualities which he received at birth render reflection less necessary; thus species endowed with some powerful instinct seem not to be intelligent when they live sheltered from unforeseen events.

From one point of view instinct appears to be a degradation rather than a perfecting of intelligence, because the acts which proceed from it are neither so spontaneous nor so personal; but from another point of view they are much better executed, with less hesitation, with a slighter expenditure of cerebral force and a minimum of muscular effort. A habitual act costs us much less to execute than a deliberate and reflective act. It is thus that the constructions of bees are more perfect than those of ants; the former act by instinct, the latter reason their acts at each step.

*Instinctive actions originate in reflective actions.*—No doubt it may be said: It is a pure hypothesis thus to consider instinct as derived from intelligence; why not admit as well that instinctive acts have been such from the beginning—in other words, that species have been created such as we see them to-day? The preceding explanation, however, has the advantage of being in harmony with the general theory of evolution, which, whether true or not, so well explains the most complicated facts that for the present it must be accepted. For the rest, if it is not possible to appraise the psychic faculties possessed by the ancestors of existing animals we may at least observe certain facts which put us on the road of explanation.

An interesting member of the Hymenoptera, the *Sphex*, assures food for the early days of the life of its larvæ in a curious way.[1] Before laying its eggs it seizes a cricket, paralyses it with two strokes of its sting—one at the articulation of the head and the neck, the other at the articulation of the first ring of the thorax with the second—each stab traversing and poisoning a nervous ganglion. The cricket is paralysed without being killed; its flesh does not putrefy, and yet it makes no movement. The *Sphex* places an egg on this motionless prey, and the larva which emerges from it devours the cricket. Here assuredly is a marvellous and certain instinct. One cannot even object that the strokes of the sting are inevitably directed to these points because the chitinous envelope of the victim offers too much resistance in

[1] "Étude sur l'Instinct et les Metamorphoses des Sphégiens," *Ann. Sc. Nat.*, iv. Série, t. 6, 1856.

other spots for the dart to penetrate, because here is the *Ammophila*, a near relative of the *Sphex*, which chooses for its prey a caterpillar. It is free to introduce its sting into any part of the body, and yet with extreme certainty it strikes the two ganglions already mentioned.[1]

We cannot suppose that the insect has anatomical and physiological knowledge to inform it of what it is doing. The act is distinctly instinctive, and seems imprinted by a fatality involving no possible connection with intelligence. But let us suppose that the ancestors of these Hymenoptera have thus attacked crickets and killed (not paralysed) them with one or more wounds at any point. By chance some of these insects, either in consequence of their manner of attacking the prey or from any other cause, happen to deliver their blows at the points in question. Their larvæ on this account are placed in more favourable conditions than those of their relatives whom chance has less well served; they will prosper and develop sooner. They inherit this habit, which gradually becomes through the ages that which we know. It is possible; but why, it may be asked, this hypothesis, apparently gratuitous, of strokes of the sting given at random? Are there any facts which render this explanation plausible? Assuredly. Thus the *Bembex*, which especially attacks Diptera to make them the prey of its larvæ, throws itself suddenly on them and kills them with one blow in any part of the body. It is unable in this way to amass in advance sufficient provision for its larvæ; the corpses would putrefy.

[1] P. Marchal, "Observations sur *l'Ammophila affinis*," *Arch. de Zool. expér. et génér.*, ii. Série, t. 10, 1892.

It is obliged to return from time to time bearing new pasture.[1] Again, M. Paul Marchal, taking up the study of instinct in the *Cerceris ornata*,[2] has shown that in this species at least of *Sphegidæ* the stings have not so considerable an effect. This insect attacks a wild bee, the *Halictus*. He strikes his victim with two or three strokes of the sting beneath the thorax, but the paralysis is not definite, perhaps on account of the nature of the venom, which is not identical in all species. The tortured creature may regain life at the end of some hours. Thus the *Cerceris* is obliged to destroy the upper part of the neck by repeated malaxation of that part for several minutes at a time. The effect of this second act, by injuring the cerebroid ganglia, is to render impossible the return of action; moreover, it permits the aggressor to satisfy personal gluttony, and to feed on the liquids of the organism of the vanquished, which is easy, because the dorsal blood-vessel passes at this level. It can thus satisfy a personal need while thinking of the future of the race.

It has been said in this connection that in such cases the sure instinct with which these species were originally endowed has been distorted, but that is to admit some degree of variation; the hypothesis of degeneration is as gratuitous as the other, and if we go so far as to risk a hypothesis, it would be better to use it to explain facts and not to entangle them.

*Plan of study of the various industries.*—The different industries carried on by animals may be divided into a certain number of groups. In the case

[1] J. H. Fabre, *Souvenirs entomologiques*, pp. 225 *et seq.*

[2] "Étude sur l'Instinct du *Cerceris ornata*," *Archives de Zoologie expérimentale*, ii. Série, t. 5, 1887.

of each of these categories I propose to arrange the facts in such a way as to bring forward first those animals which, having no special organs, are obliged to exercise the greatest ingenuity, and then to indicate the facts which show how variations have arisen which enable other species to accomplish these acts with marvellous ease.

We will first examine the simplest industries: hunting and fishing, those industries of which the object is the immediate search for prey; and to these may be added those which are related to them as re-action is to action—that is to say, the industries of which the effect is to provide for the immediate safety of the individual.

Then in an exposition parallel to the march of progress followed by human civilisations, we shall study among animals the art of collecting provisions, of domesticating and exploiting flocks, of reducing their fellows to slavery.

Finally, we shall investigate the series of modifications which the dwelling undergoes, and we shall see how certain species, after having constructed admirably-arranged houses, know how to make them healthy, and how to defend them against attacks from without.

# CHAPTER II.

## HUNTING—FISHING—WARS AND EXPEDITIONS.

THE CARNIVORA MORE SKILFUL HUNTERS THAN THE HERBIVORA—DIFFERENT METHODS OF HUNTING—HUNTING IN AMBUSH—THE BAITED AMBUSH—HUNTING IN THE DWELLING OR IN THE BURROW—COURSING—STRUGGLES THAT TERMINATE THE HUNT—HUNTING WITH PROJECTILES—PARTICULAR CIRCUMSTANCES PUT TO PROFIT—METHODS FOR UTILISING THE CAPTURED GAME—WAR AND BRIGANDAGE—EXPEDITIONS TO ACQUIRE SLAVES—WARS OF THE ANTS.

*The Carnivora more skilful hunters than the Herbivora.*—The search for food has necessarily been the cause of the earliest industries among animals. It is easy to understand that the herbivora need little ingenuity in seeking nourishment; they are so superior to their prey that they can obtain it and feed on it by the sole fact of an organisation adapted to its assimilation. They are, it is true, at the mercy of circumstances over which they have no control, and which lead to famine. The carnivora also may have to suffer from the absence of prey, but even in the most favourable seasons, and in the regions where the animals on which they live abound, it is necessary to them to develop a special activity to obtain possession of beings who are suspicious, prompt in flight, and as fleet as themselves. Thus it is among these that we expect to find the art of hunting most cultivated; especially if we put aside the more grossly carnivorous of them, whose whole organisation is adapted for rapid and effective results.

*Different methods of hunting.*—Like Man, some animals hunt in ambush or by coursing; others know how to overturn the desired victim by throwing some object at it. These profit by all the exterior circumstances which are capable of frightening the game, of stunning it, and of rendering capture easy. But it is by studying each separate feature that we shall best be able to observe the close way in which these industries are related to our own. It is impossible to bring forward all the facts relating to the search for prey among animals; we can only take a few as sign-posts which mark the road.

*Hunting in ambush.*—The most rudimentary method of hunting in ambush is simply to take advantage of some favourable external circumstance to obtain concealment, and then to await the approach of the prey. Some animals place themselves behind a tuft of grass, others thrust themselves into a thicket, or hang on to the branch of a tree in order to fall suddenly on the victim who innocently approaches the perfidious ambush. The Crocodile, as described by Sir Samuel Baker, conceals himself by his skill in plunging noiseelssly. On the bank a group of birds have alighted. They search the mud for insects or worms, or simply to approach the stream to drink or bathe. In spite of his great size and robust appetite the Crocodile does not disdain this slight dish; but the least noise, the least wrinkle on the surface of the water would cause the future repast to vanish. The reptile plunges, the birds continue without suspicion to come and go. Suddenly there emerges before them the huge open jaw armed with formidable teeth. In the moment of stupor and immobility which this unforeseen apparition produces a few imprudent birds have disappeared within the reptile's mouth, while the others fly away. In the same sly and brutal manner he snaps up dogs, horses, oxen, and even men who come to the river to drink.

One of the most dangerous ambushes which can be met on the road by animals who resort to a spring is that prepared by the Python. This gigantic snake hangs by his tail to the branch of a tree and lets himself droop down like a long creeper. The victim who comes within his reach is seized, enrolled, pounded in the knots which the snake forms around him. It is not necessary to multiply examples of this simple and widespread method of hunting.

Not content with utilising the natural arrangements they meet with, there are animals which construct genuine ambushes, acting thus like Man, who builds in the middle or on the edge of ponds, cabins in which to await wild ducks, or who digs in the path of a lion a hole covered with trunks of trees, at the bottom of which he may kill the beast without danger. Certain insects practise this method of hunting. The Fox, for instance, so skilful a hunter in many respects, constructs an ambush when hunting hares.[1]

The larva of the Tiger Beetle (*Cicindela campestris*) constructs a hole about the size of a feather quill, disposed vertically, and of a depth, enormous for its size, of forty centimetres. It maintains itself in this tube by arching its supple body along the walls at a

[1] C. St. John, *Wild Sports, etc.*, chap. xx.

height sufficient for the top of its head to be level with the surface of the soil, and to close the opening of the hole. (Fig. 1.) A little insect—an ant, a young beetle, or something similar—passes. As soon as it begins to walk on the head of the larva, the latter letting go its hold of the wall allows itself to fall to the bottom of the trap, dragging its victim with it. In this narrow prison it is easily able to obtain the mastery over its prey, and to suck out the liquid parts.[1]

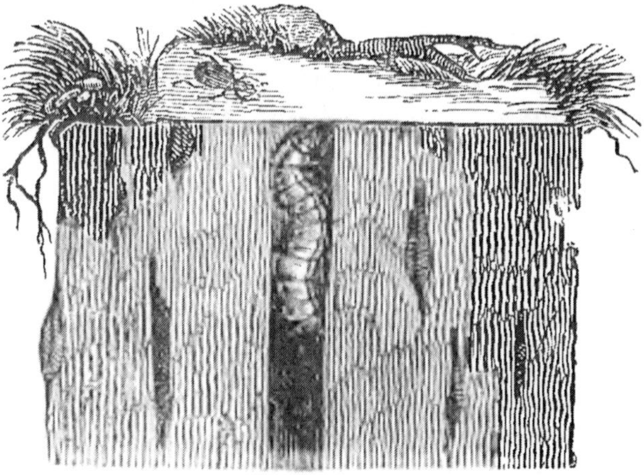

FIG. 1.

The *Staphilinus Cæsareus* acts with still greater shrewdness; not only is his pit more perfect, but he takes care to remove all traces of preceding repasts which might render the place obviously one of carnage. He chooses a stone, beneath which he hollows a cylindro-conical hole with extremely smooth walls. This hole is not to serve as a trap,

[1] Lamarck, *Histoire des Animaux sans Vertèbres*, 2e édition, 1835, p. 676.

that is to say that the proprietor has no intention of causing any pedestrian to roll to the bottom. It is simply a place of concealment in which he awaits the propitious moment. No creature is more patient than this insect, and no delay discourages him. As soon as some small animal approaches his hiding-place he throws himself on it impetuously, kills it, and devours it. Near his ditch he has hollowed a second of a much coarser character, the walls of which have not been smoothed with the same care. One here sees elytra and claws piled up; they are the hard and horny parts which he has not been able to eat. The heap in this ditch is not then an alimentary store. It is the *oubliette* in which the *Staphilinus* buries the remains of his victims. If he allowed them to accumulate around his hole all pedestrians would come to fear this spot and to avoid it. It would be like the dwelling of a Polypus, which is marked by the numerous carapaces of crabs and shells which strew the neighbourhood.

The ambuscade of the Ant-lion is classic; it does not differ greatly from the others. He excavates a conical pitfall, in which he conceals himself, and seizes the unfortunate ants and other insects whom ill-chance causes to roll into it.[1]

*The baited ambush.*—A variety of ambush which brings this method of hunting to considerable perfection lies in inciting the prey to approach the hiding-place instead of trusting to chance to bring it there. In such circumstances Man places some allurement in the neighbourhood—that is to say, one of the foods preferred by the desired victim, or at

[1] See *e.g.* Tennent, *Ceylon*, vol. i. p. 252. Also Réaumur, *Mémoires pour d'histoire des Insectes*, t. i. p. 14, and t. vi. p. 333.

least some object which recalls the form of that food, as, for example, an artificial fly to obtain possession of certain fishes.

It is curious to find that fish themselves utilise this system; it is the method adopted by the Angler and the *Uranoscopus*.[1] The *Urañoscopus scaber* lives in the Mediterranean. At the end of his lower jaw there is developed a mobile and supple filament which he is able to use with the greatest dexterity. Concealed in the mud, without moving and only allowing the end of his head to emerge, he agitates and vibrates his filament. The little fishes who prowl in the neighbourhood, delighted with the sight of this apparent worm, regarding it as a destined prey, throw themselves on to it, but before they are able to bite and recognise their error they have disappeared in the mouth of the proprietor of the bait.

The Angler (*Lophius piscatorius*) has not usurped his rather paradoxical name. He retires to the midst of the sea-weed and algæ. On his body and all round his head he bears fringed appendages which, by their resemblance to the leaves of marine plants, aid the animal to conceal himself. The colour of his body also does not contrast with neighbouring objects. From his head arise three movable filaments formed by three spines detached from the upper fin. He makes use of the anterior one, which is the longest and most supple. Working in the same way as the *Uranoscopus*, the Angler agitates his three filaments, giving them as much as possible the appearance of worms, and thus attracting the little fish on which he feeds.

In these two examples we see a special organ

1 Lacepède, *Histoire des Poissons*, 1798-1803.

utilised for a particular function; it is one of the intermediate cases, already referred to, between the true industries involving ingenuity and the simple phenomena due to adaptations and modifications of the body.

*Hunting in the dwelling or in the burrow.*—All these methods of hunting or of fishing by surprise are for the most part practised by the less agile species which cannot obtain their prey by superior fleetness. Midway between these two methods may be placed that which consists in surprising game when some circumstance has rendered it motionless. Sometimes it is sleep which places it at the mercy of the hunter, whose art in this case consists in seeking out its dwelling. Sometimes he profits by the youth of the victim, like all bird-nesters, whose aim is to eat the eggs or to devour the young while still incapable of flying. The animals who eat birds' eggs are numerous both among mammals and reptiles, as well as among birds themselves.

The Alligator of Florida and of Louisiana delights in this chase. He seeks in particular the Great Boat-Tail (*Quiscalus major*) which nests in the reeds at the edge of marshes and ponds. When the young have come out and are expecting from their parents the food which the chances of the hunt may delay, they do not cease chirping and calling by their cries. But the parents are not alone in hearing these appeals. They may also strike the ears of the alligator, who furtively approaches the imprudent singers. With a sudden stroke of his tail he strikes the reeds and throws into the water one or more of the hungry young ones, who are then at his mercy. (Audubon.)

The animals who feed on species living in societies either seize on their prey when isolated or when all the members of the colony are united in their city. A search for the nest is necessary in the case of creatures who are very small in comparison with the hunter, as in the case of ants and the Ant-eater. But the ant-eater possesses a very long and sticky tongue, which renders the capture of these insects extremely easy; when he finds a frequented passage it is enough to stretch out his tongue; all the ants come of their own accord and place themselves on it, and when it is sufficiently charged he withdraws it and devours them. The African *Orycteropus* (Fig. 2), who is also a great eater of ants and especially of termites, is equally aided by a very developed tongue; but he has less patience than the ant-eater, and he adds to this resource other proceedings which render the hunt more fruitful and enable him to obtain a very large number of insects at one time. Thanks to his keenness of scent he soon discovers an ant-path bearing the special and characteristic odour which these Hymenoptera leave behind them, and he follows the track which leads to their nest. On arriving there, without troubling himself about the scattered insects that prowl in the neighbourhood, he sets himself to penetrate into the midst of the dwelling, and with his strong claws hollows out a passage which enables him to gain access. On the way he pierces walls, breaks down floors, gathering here and there some fugitives, and arrives at last at the centre, in which millions of animals swarm. He then swallows them in large mouthfuls and retires, leaving behind him a desert and a ruin in the spot before occupied by a veritable palace, full of prodigious activity.

The colonies are not only exposed to the devastations of those who feed on their members; they have other enemies in the animals who covet their stores

FIG. 2.

of food. The most inveterate robber of bees is the nocturnal Death's Head Moth. When he has succeeded in penetrating the hive the stings of the proprietors who throw themselves on him do not trouble him, thanks to his thick fleece of long hairs which the sting cannot penetrate; he makes his way to the cells, rips them open, gorges himself with honey, and causes such havoc that in Switzerland, in certain years when these butterflies were abundant, numbers of hives have been found absolutely empty.[1] Many other marauders and of larger size, such as the Bear, also spread terror among these laborious insects and empty their barns. No animal is more crafty than the Raven, and the fabulist who wished to make him a dupe was obliged to oppose to him the very cunning Fox in order to render the tale fairly life-like. A great number of stories are told concerning the Raven's cleverness, and many of them are undoubtedly true. There is no bolder robber of nests. He swallows the eggs and eats the little ones of the species who cannot defend themselves against him; he even seeks the eggs of Sea-gulls on the coast; but in this case he must use cunning, for if he is discovered it means a serious battle. On the coast also the Raven seeks to obtain possession of the Hermit-crab. This Crustacean dwells in the empty shells of Gasteropods. At the least alarm he retires within this shell and becomes invisible, but the bird advances with so much precaution that he is often able to seize the crab before he has time to hide himself. If the raven fails he turns the shell over and over until the impatient crustacean allows a claw to emerge; he is then seized and immediately devoured.

If there is a question of hunting larger game like a Hare, the Raven prefers to take an ally. They start him at his burrow and pursue him flying. In spite of his proverbial rapidity the hare is scarcely able to

[1] Huber, *Nouvelles Observations sur les Abeilles*, t. ii. p. 291.

flee more than two hundred yards. He succumbs beneath vigorous blows on his skull from the beaks of his assailants. During winter, in the high regions of the Alps, when the soil is covered with snow, this chase is particularly fruitful for ravens. The story is told of that unfortunate hare who had hollowed out in the snow a burrow with two entrances. Two of these birds having recognised his presence, one entered one hole in order to dislodge the hare, the other awaited him at the other opening to batter his head with blows from his beak and kill him before he had time to gain presence of mind.[1]

Rooks sometimes hunt in burrows by ingeniously-concerted operations. Mr. Bernard[2] has described the interesting way in which the Rook hunts voles or field-mice in Thuringia. His curiosity was excited by the way in which numerous rooks stood about a field cawing loudly. In a few days this was explained: the field was covered with rooks; the original assemblage had been calling together a mouse-hunt, which could only be successfully carried out by a large number of birds acting in conjunction. By diligently probing the ground and blocking up the network of runs, the voles, one or more at a time, were gradually driven into a corner. The hunt was very successful, and no more voles were seen in that field during the winter.

*Coursing.*—Other animals are not easily discouraged by the swiftness of their prey; they count on their own resistance in order to tire the game; some of them also manage their pursuit in the most intelligent way, so as to preserve their own strength while the

[1] F. von Tschüdi, *Les Alpes*, Berne and Paris, 1859.

[2] *Zoologist*, October 1892.

tracked animal's strength goes on diminishing until exhaustion and fatigue place him at their mercy.

Mammals especially, such as Dogs, Wolves, and Foxes, exercise this kind of chase; it is, exactly, the coursing which Man has merely had to direct for his own benefit. Wild dogs pursue their prey united in immense packs. They excite each other by barking while they frighten the game and half paralyse his efforts. No animal is agile and strong enough to be sure of escaping. They surround him and cut off his retreat in a most skilful manner; Gazelles and Antelopes, in spite of their extreme nimbleness and speed, are caught at last; Boars are rapidly driven into a corner; their vigorous defence may cost the life of some of the assailants, but they nevertheless become the prey of the band who rush on to the quarry. In Asia wild dogs do not fear even to attack the tiger. Many no doubt are crushed by a blow of the animal's paw or strangled in his jaws, but the death of comrades does not destroy either the courage or the greediness of the surviving aggressors. Their number also is such that the great beast, covered by agile enemies who cling to him and wound him in every part, must at last succumb.

Wolves hunt also in considerable bands. Their audacity, especially when pressed by hunger in the bad season, is well known. In time of war they follow armies, to attack stragglers and to devour the dead. In Siberia they pursue sledges on the snow with terrible perseverance, and the pack is not delayed by the massacre of those who are shot. A few stop to devour at once their fallen comrades, while the others continue the pursuit.

Besides these brutal chases wolves seem able to

exercise a genuine feint. Sometimes it is a couple who hunt in concert. If they meet a flock, as they are well aware that the dog will bravely defend the animals entrusted to him, that he is vigilant, and that his keen scent will bring him on them much sooner than the shepherd, it is with him that they first occupy themselves. The two wolves approach secretly; then suddenly one of them unmasks and attracts the attention of the dog, who rushes after him with such ardour that he fails to perceive that in the meantime the second thief has seized the sheep and dragged it into the wood. The dog finally renounces his pursuit of the fugitive and returns to his flock. Then the two confederates join each other and share the prey. In other circumstances it is a wolf who hunts with his female. When they wish to obtain possession of a deer, whose robust flight may last a long time, one of the couple, the male for example, pursues him and directs his chase in such a way that the game must pass by a place where the female wolf is concealed. She then takes up the chase while the male reposes. It is an organised system of relays. The strength of the deer becomes necessarily exhausted; he cannot resist the animation shown by his active foe, and is seized and killed. Then the other wolf calmly approaches the place of the feast to share his part of the booty.

The small but bold Hawk called the Merlin also courses in relays in exactly the same manner. These birds pursue a Lark or a Swallow in the most systematic manner. First one Merlin chases the bird for a short time, while his companion hovers quietly at hand; then the latter relieves his fellow-hunter, who rests in his turn. The victim is soon tired out and caught in mid-air by one of the Merlins, who flies away with him, leaving his companion to hunt alone, while he feeds the young brood.[1]

The Fox also successfully uses this method of coursing with relays. There are indeed few animals who possess so many tricks of all kinds to gain possession of their prey Constantly prowling about the fields, he neglects no propitious circumstance, and profits by all the advantages furnished by the situation of places or the habits of the game he is seeking. He pursues tired or wounded animals whom he meets, and easily masters them. If he finds a burrow, he quickly hollows a hole and brings to light the young rabbits who thought themselves in safety in the bowels of the earth; he robs nests placed in the thickets, and devours the young birds. Beehives are not protected against his greediness by the stings of the swarms; he rolls on the earth, crushes his assailants, and finally triumphs over the discouraged insects and gorges himself with honey.

Birds of prey also invent ingenious combinations to reach a good flier. Most of the great rapacious birds of rapid flight or with powerful talons are so well organised for the chase that they have no need of cunning. To see the prey, to seize it and devour it, are acts accomplished in a moment by the single fact of their natural organisation. It is rather among those who are less well endowed that one finds real art and frequent ruses. The Goshawk (*Astur palumbarius*, Fig. 3) is sufficiently strong and flies sufficiently well to seize small birds; but in order to obtain a copious repast at one snatch he prefers to

[1] C. St. John, *Wild Sports and Natural History of the Highlands*, chap. xi.

FIG. 3.

attack pigeons. Generally the strength of their wings promptly places them in safety. He therefore hides himself in the neighbourhood of the pigeon-house, ready to fall on those pigeons who pick up food around. But the pigeons are suspicious, and if they recognise his presence they remain hidden in their dwellings. In this case it has sometimes been found that the Goshawk has quietly flown up to their house and alighted on its summit; there, by violently beating his wings, he gives a succession of sudden blows to the roof. Startled and frightened by this unaccustomed noise, the inhabitants dart out, and the bird of prey can then profit by their alarm to seize one or two.[1]

The *Pseudaetus* is also obliged to have recourse to a subterfuge in order to gain birds that fly well. He easily destroys fowls, and hunts them so successfully that in Spain, in certain isolated farms, it has been necessary to give up rearing fowls in consequence of these numerous depredations. But to seize pigeons is not so easy a matter. Generally, according to Jerdon, two birds unite to attack a band. One of the aggressors pretends to wish to seize them from below. This is a very unusual method, for birds of prey always rise above the game in order to throw themselves down on it. This puts out the pigeons, and they fear the manœuvre all the more because they are unaccustomed to it. During this instant of confusion the second assailant passes unperceived above them, plunges into the midst and seizes a pigeon; there is a new panic, by which the first aggressor profits in order to rise rapidly in his turn and seize a second victim.

[1] Wodzicki, "Ornithologische Miscell.," *Journ. f. Ornithol.*, 1856.

*Struggles that terminate the hunt.*—It is not always sufficient for the hunter to find game and to reach it. If the game is of large size it may be able to hold its own, and the pursuit may end in a violent struggle, in which both skill and cunning are necessary to obtain conquest.

The Bald Eagle of North America (*Haliäetus leucocephalus*) hides himself on a rock by the edge of a stream and awaits the passing of a swan. This eagle is brave and strong, but the palmiped is vigorous, and though inferior in the air, he has an advantage on the water, and may escape death by plunging. The eagle knows this advantage, so he compels the swan to remain in the air by attacking him from below and repeatedly striking his belly. Weakened by the flow of blood, and obliged to fly, not being able to reach the water without finding the sharp beak which strikes him, the swan succumbs in this unequal combat, which has been vividly described by Audubon.

The bird who displays the most remarkable qualities in this struggle which terminates the chase, exhibiting indeed a real fencing match, is the Secretary Bird (*Gypogeranus reptilivorus.* Fig. 4.) He is the more interested in striking without being himself struck since the fangs with which his prey, the snake, is generally armed might at the first blow give him a mortal wound. In South Africa he pursues every snake, even the most venomous. Warned by instinct of the terrible enemy he has met, the reptile at first seeks safety in flight; the Secretary follows him on foot, and the ardour of the chase does not prevent him from being constantly on guard. This is because the snake, finding himself nearly overtaken, suddenly turns round, ready to use his defensive weapons. The bird stops, and turns in one of his wings to protect the lower parts of his body. A real duel then begins. The snake throws himself on his enemy, who at each stroke parries

FIG. 4.

with the end of his wing; the fangs are buried in the great feathers which terminate it, and there leave their poison without producing any effect. All this time with the other wing the Secretary repeatedly strikes the reptile, who is at last stunned, and rolls over on the earth. The conqueror rapidly thrusts his beak into his skull, throws his victim into the air, and swallows him.[1]

*Hunting with projectiles.*—It has often been repeated that Man is the only creature sufficiently intelligent to utilise as weapons exterior objects like a stone or a stick; in a much greater degree, therefore, it was said, was he the only creature capable of striking from afar with a projectile. Nevertheless creatures so inferior as fish exhibit extreme skill in the art of reaching their prey at a distance. Several act in this way. There is first the *Toxotes jaculator*, who lives in the rivers of India. His principal food is formed by the insects who wander over the leaves of aquatic plants. To wait until they fell into the water would naturally result in but meagre fare. To leap at them with one bound is difficult, not to mention that the noise would cause them to flee. The *Toxotes* knows a better trick than that. He draws in some drops of water, and, contracting his mouth, projects them with so much force and certainty that they rarely fail to reach the chosen aim, and to bring into the water all the insects he desires.[2] (Fig. 5.) Other animals also squirt various liquids, sometimes in attack, but more especially in defence. The Cephalopods, for example, emit their ink, which darkens the water and allows them to flee. Certain insects exude bitter or fœtid liquids; but in all these cases, and in others that are similar, the

[1] The combat was minutely described by Le Vaillant (*Hist. Nat. des Oiseaux d'Afrique*, Paris, 1798, t. i. p. 177), whose account has been confirmed by many subsequent observers.

[2] Cuvier et Valenciennes, *Hist. Nat. des Poissons*, Paris, 1831, t. vii. p. 231.

Fig. 5.

animal finds in his own organism a secretion which happens to be more or less useful to his conservation. The method of the *Toxotes* is different. It is a foreign body which he takes up, and it is an intended victim at which he takes aim and which he strikes; his movements are admirably co-ordinated to obtain a precise effect.

Another fish, the *Chelinous* of Java, also acts in this manner. He generally lives in estuaries. It is therefore a brackish water which he takes up and projects by closing his gills and contracting his mouth; he can thus strike a fly at a distance of several feet. Usually he aims sufficiently well to strike it at the first blow, but sometimes he fails. Then he begins again until he has succeeded, which shows that his movements are not those of a machine. He knows what he is doing, what effect ought to be produced, and whether this desired result has happened, and he perseveres until the insect has fallen. These facts are unquestioned; the Chinese preserve these curious fish in jars, and amuse themselves by making them carry on this little exercise. Many observers have witnessed and described it.

*Particular circumstances put to profit.*—In the various kinds of hunting which we have been passing in review, it is certain that the animals in question generally exercise them nearly always in the same manner. If an animal has carried out a ruse successfully he does not abandon it, but reproduces it as often as it is efficacious. When, however, conditions happen to change, animals are prompt to profit by them, and one sees how all these acts are derived from reflection. This is the clearer the more the favourable circumstance is accidental and unforeseen, when it is not possible to consider the animals as accustomed to profit by it.

In the wild regions of Africa it happens that from some reason or another, perhaps from the effect of lightning on immense forests, dense thickets or plains covered by tall plants become the prey of gigantic fires which spread as long as they find food on their road. The heat as of a furnace arises above and around; an acrid smoke veils everything, and the frightened animals flee before the scourge. Travellers who have witnessed these magnificent scenes often insist on the panics thus produced, and describe the inoffensive lion fleeing in the midst of a herd of gazelles. All are seized by the same fear, because all are exposed to the same danger. But birds, whose wings can carry them at will afar from the furnace, preserve greater presence of mind, and profit by the public calamity and general anxiety to make a successful hunt and copious feasts. One may see the birds of prey flying in front of the fire and seizing easy victims. Certain birds of Africa are the most furious hunters during a fire. Legions of insects flee far from the tall dried plants, and clouds of birds arrive to throw themselves on them. They pursue them with incredible audacity through the smoke close to the flames and always retire in time to avoid singeing. A member of the Crow family who inhabits India, *Anomalocorax splendens*, enjoys a deserved reputation of astuteness and allows no opportunity to escape without seizing it by the forelock. In ordinary times his food is composed of very varied substances—crabs, insects, worms, etc.; but if he perceives afar an ascending cloud he immediately abandons his small researches, knowing there is something better to be done over there. He is not selfish, and he calls a few comrades and they all put themselves into position to await events. They know very well the relation that exists between this smoke and the prey they covet. The fire indicated by the smoke can have no other reason in this hot country than the cooking of food. A Hindoo family are in fact installed and preparing their repast. The birds see all this and observe. The Hindoos are accustomed to throw outside the remains of their meals, and the *Anomalocorax*, who have come together from afar to await patiently this result, then throw themselves on the quarry. (Jerdon.)

Tennent narrates a singular trick which was twice, to his knowledge, played on a dog by two of these small glossy crows of Ceylon. The dog was gnawing a bone and would not be disturbed from the pure delight of sucking the marrow of which he was the legitimate proprietor. A crow approached the scene of the feast, and conceived the design of taking possession of it; he began by hopping around the dog, going and coming, trying to attract the animal's attention and ready to profit by the first distraction. His gambols remaining without result, he understood that he would not succeed and he flew away; but it was only to return accompanied by a friend possessing as little respect as himself for the property of others. The associate perched on a branch a few steps away, while the first crow renewed his attempts by flying around the bone and the dog; but the latter remained impassive. Then the second personage, whose part had hitherto been to remain contemplative, flew off his branch, threw himself on the dog and gave him a formidable blow on the spine. Seized with indignation, the dog turned round to punish the author of this unjustifiable aggression; but the bird was already far away, and in the meanwhile from the other side the first *Anomalocorax* seized the long-coveted bone and also took flight. The feelings of the sheepish dog who saw both his vengeance and his repast flying away in the air may be better imagined than described.[1]

All the birds, indeed, of this family know how to reach their ends. I have already spoken of certain hunts of the Raven; it is even said that in Iceland he knows when a ewe is going to give birth to young, and awaits this moment with immense patience. As soon as the lamb appears the Raven alights on him, digs out his eyes, and devours them.

The Quelelis or Guadaloupe Caracara (*Polyborus lutosus*), a Californian bird of prey, is a cruel enemy to animals like the goat when they are about to bring forth their young. No sooner is one kid born, and while the mother is yet in labour with the second, than the birds pounce upon it, and should the mother be able to interfere, she is assaulted also. If there are a number of young kids together, the birds unite their forces and with great noise and flapping of wings succeed in separating the weakest and killing it.[2]

Dr. J. Lowe has recently called attention to a very curious method of attracting prey adopted by the Blackcap (*Sylvia atricapilla*) at Orotava, Teneriffe.[3] This bird has discovered that the juice exuded by certain flowers (*Hibiscus Rosa sinensis* and *Abutilon frondosum*) is attractive to the insects upon which

[1] Tennent, *Ceylon*, vol. i. p. 171.

[2] Bendire, *Life Histories of North American Birds*, 1892, p. 319.

[3] Linnæan Society, 1st June 1893.

he preys; he therefore punctures the petals of these flowers in order to promote the exudation of this viscid secretion.

Many of us in our schooldays have admired the intelligence of Jackdaws having their nests in some old tower or belfry. They are able to distinguish according to the hour the significance of the various school bells. Most of these clangs do not move them, and they continue to attend to their affairs without paying attention. Their attention is only attracted by the ringing which marks the beginning and the end of recreation time. At the sound of the first they all flee and abandon the courts before even a single pupil has yet appeared. The bell, on the contrary, which marks the end of recreation time invites them to descend in a band to collect the crumbs of lunch. They arrive in a hurry, so as to be the first to profit by the repast, not waiting even until the place is abandoned; they know very well that the young people still there are not to be feared, having no time now to be occupied with them.

In this class of facts, there are a certain number which may be considered as more marked by custom and perhaps less marked by spontaneous reflection. Such, for example, is the custom of Sharks and Sea-gulls to follow ships.

In the seas where Dog-fish are abundant, one or more of them become attached to a ship, and quit it neither night nor day. One may believe sometimes that they are not there; but if any object is thrown into the sea, the fin of one of these monsters appears at the surface; everything which is thrown overboard disappears in their large jaws—kitchen refuse, bottles, etc. When a dead body is thrown into the sea it is soon seized by the shark, while living men who fall into the water have great difficulty in escaping, and are often drawn up horribly mutilated and half dead.

Sea-gulls also follow vessels when they approach the coast. It is a pleasant sight to see the noisy band animating the monotonous splendour of the ocean; they arrive as soon as a vessel is one or two days' journey from land. Henceforth they do not leave her, flying behind and plunging in her wake; they profit by the disturbance produced by the gigantic machine to capture the stunned fishes.

On land exactly the same kind of chase is carried on by Rooks, Crows, and Magpies, who follow the plough to seize the worms which the ploughshare turns up in the open earth. In autumn they cover the fields, animated and active, pilfering as the furrow is hollowed out.

Certain rapacious birds who are awkward in hunting, especially Kites, make up for their lack of skill by audacious impudence. Constantly on the watch for better hunters like the Falcon, they throw themselves on him as soon as he has seized his prey. The proud bird, though much more courageous, stronger, and more skilful than these thieves, usually abandons the prey either because the burden embarrasses him in the struggle, or else because he knows that he can easily find another. These highway robbers of the air often unite to gain possession of a prey already taken and killed, and ready to be eaten. A handsome Falcon of the Southern States of North America, the Caracara Eagle (*Polyborus cheriway*), frequently steals fish from the Brown Pelicans on the coast of Texas. When the Pelicans are returning from their expeditions with pouches filled with fish, the Caracaras attack them until they disgorge, and then alight to devour the stolen prey. They do not attack the outgoing birds, but only the incoming ones, and they wait until they reach the land (so that the contents of the pouches may not fall into the water) before pouncing on them.[1]

Among other animals a habit has been formed from some special circumstance. As an extreme case in this group we meet with parasites of whom some cannot live outside a particular nest, and are even absolutely transformed by this kind of life. But between these and independent hunters there are an extreme number of intermediate stages, of which it is sufficient to mention a few.[2]

The *Fierasfer*, a little fish of the Mediterranean, installs himself in the respiratory cavity of a Holothurian; he does not live at the expense of his host's flesh, but contents himself with levying a tax on the foods which enter the cavity. It is a case of commensalism of which there are very numerous examples. Other cases may be mentioned which are still further removed from parasitism. Among these may be mentioned the birds who relieve large mammals of their vermin.

One of them, the Red-beaked Buffalo bird (*Buphaga erythrorhyncha*), lives in Abyssinia. This bird is insectivorous. He has remarked that the ruminants constitute baits for flies; therefore he never leaves these animals, hops about on their backs and delivers them from annoying parasites; the buffaloes, who

[1] Bendire, *Life Histories of North American Birds*, p. 315.

[2] For a discussion of this subject, see P. van Beneden, *Commensaux et Parasites*, Paris, 1875.

recognise this service, allow the bird to wander quietly over their hide. The *Buphaga*, who gives himself up entirely to this kind of chase, is often called the Beef-eater. He is only found in the society of flocks, of camels, buffaloes, or oxen. He settles on the back, legs, and snouts of these living baits. They remain passive even when he opens the skin in order to draw out the flies' larva ; they know the benefit of this little operation. The patience of the oxen is certainly due to custom, for it is observed that herds which are not used to this bird manifest great terror when he prepares to alight on them, so that they even take flight from this small aggressor.

Sometimes it is not easy to understand the advantages derived by the animal from the conditions in which he is usually found. Thus, for example, there is a fish, the *Polyprion cernium*, which accompanies driftwood on which Barnacles have fixed themselves. Yet the remains of these Crustaceans are never found in his stomach, and it is known on the contrary that he lives exclusively on other small fish. It is possible that these find their food in fragments of wood at the expense of the barnacles, and that therefore the *Polyprion* which hunts them is always near driftwood thus garnished.

*Methods of utilising the captured game.*—Frequently it is not enough for the animal to obtain possession of his prey. Before making his meal it is still necessary to find a method of making use of it, either because the eatable parts are buried in a thick shell which he is unable to break, or because he has captured a creature which rolls itself into a ball and bristles its plumes. Here are some of the more curious practices followed in such cases.

Sometimes it is a question of carrying off a round fruit which offers no prominence to take hold of. The Red-headed Melanerpes (*Melanerpes erythrocephalus*) of North America is very greedy with regard to apples, and feeds on them as well as on cherries. It takes him a considerable time to consume an apple, and as he is well aware of the danger he runs by prolonging his stay in an orchard, he wishes to carry away his booty to a safe and sheltered spot. He vigorously plunges his open beak into the apple; the two mandibles enter separately, and the fruit is well fixed; he detaches it and flies away to the chosen retreat. Apes are very skilful in utilising their booty. Cocoa-nuts are rather hard to open, but Apes do not lose any part of them; they first tear off the fibrous envelope with their teeth, then they enlarge the natural holes with their fingers, and drink the milk. Finally, in order to reach the kernel they strike the nut on some hard object exactly as Man would do. The Baboons (*Cynocephali*), whose courage is prodigious, since they will fight in a band against a pack of dogs or even against a leopard, are also very prudent and very skilful. They know that courage is no use against the sting of a venomous snake, and that the best thing is to avoid being bitten. The scorpion, whose dart is perfidious, also inspires their distrust, but as they like eating him they endeavour to catch him. This is not indeed very difficult if one carefully observes his movements, and it is possible to seize him suddenly by the tail, as I have often done, without being stung. Apes employ this method, pull out his sting, and crunch the now inoffensive Arachnid. They also like ants, but fear being bitten by them; when they wish to enjoy them, they place an open hand on an ant-hill and remain motionless until it is covered by insects. They can then absorb them at one stroke without fear.

One would not think that an animal so well defended as the Hedgehog need fear becoming the prey of the Fox. Rolled in a ball, bristling with hard prickles which cruelly wound an assailant's mouth, nothing will induce him to unroll so long as he supposes the enemy still in the neighbourhood. It is vain to strike him or to rub him on the earth; he remains on the armed defensive. Only one circumstance disturbs him to the point of making him quit his prudent posture; it is to feel himself in the water, or even simply to be moist. The fox is acquainted with this weakness, therefore as soon as he has captured a hedgehog he rolls him in the nearest marsh to strangle him as soon as his head appears. It may happen that there is no puddle in the neighbourhood suitable for this bath; it is said that in this case the fox is not embarrassed for so small a matter, and provides from his own body the wherewithal to moisten the hedgehog.

The combination is complicated, and approaches more nearly the methods employed by Man when the animal makes use of a foreign body, as a tool or as a fulcrum, to achieve his objects. A snake is very embarrassed when he has swallowed an entire egg with the shell; he cannot digest it in that condition, and the muscles of his stomach are not strong enough to break it. The snake often finds himself in this condition, and is then accustomed either to strike his body against hard objects or to coil himself around them until he has broken the envelope of the eggs he contains.

The Snake himself is treated in this way in South America. The Sulphur Tyrant-bird picks up a young snake by the tail, and, flying to a branch or stone, uses it like a flail until its life is battered out.[1]

It would be a paradox to attribute great intelligence to Batrachians; yet certain facts are recorded which show them to be capable of reflection. Among others the case is quoted of a green frog who obtained possession of a small red frog, and who proposed to swallow him. The other was naturally opposed to the realisation of this scheme and struggled with energy. Seeing that he would not succeed, the green frog went towards the trunk of a tree and, still holding his victim, struck him many times vigorously against it. At last the red frog was stunned, and could then be swallowed at leisure.

Gasteropods are not always protected by their calcareous shells any more than tortoises are by their carapaces; for certain birds know very well how to break them. Ravens drop snails from a height, and thus get possession of the contents of the shell.

The most celebrated breaker of shells is the Bearded Vulture or Lammergeyer (*Gypäetos barbatus*). This rapacious bird is very common in Greece, where he does not usually live on large prey. If he sometimes carries away a fowl, it is exceptional; he prefers to live on carrion or bones, the remains of the feasts of man or of the true vulture. He rises very high carrying these bones in his talons and allows them to fall on a stone, swallowing the fragments after having sucked out the marrow. He is also greedy of tortoises, and uses the same method to break their

[1] W. H. Hudson, *Naturalist in La Plata*, p. 73.

carapaces, eating the soft parts. These facts have been many times observed by Brehm and other trustworthy naturalists. It is even said that in Greece every Lammergeyer chooses a rock on which he always comes to execute the tortoises he has captured. It was no doubt beneath one of these birds so occupied that, according to the story, mischance conducted Æschylus.

Neither the beak nor the claws of the Shrike or Butcher-bird (*Lanius excubitor*) are strong enough to enable him to tear his prey easily. When he is not too driven by hunger he installs himself in a comfortable fashion for this carving process, places on a thorn or on a pointed branch the victim he has made, and when it is thus fixed easily devours it in threads.

The *Lanius collurio*, an allied bird, uses this method still more frequently. He even prepares a small larder before feasting. One may thus see on a thorny branch spitted side by side Coleoptera, crickets, grasshoppers, frogs, and even young birds, which he has seized when they were in flight.[1] (Fig. 6.)

Of all these well-attested facts that which perhaps best shows how animals in certain circumstances may take advantage of a foreign body to utilise the product of the chase, is the following, the observation of which is due to Parseval-Deschênes.[2] He followed during several hours an ant bearing a heavy burden. On arriving at the foot of a little hillock the animal was unable to mount with his load, and abandoned it—a very extraordinary fact for one who knows the

[1] Naumann, *Naturgeschichte der Vögel Deutschlands, etc.*, Stuttgart, 1846-53.

[2] Gratien de Semur, *Traité des erreurs et des préjugés*, Paris, 1848, p. 70.

FIG. 6.

inconceivable tenacity of insects. The abandonment therefore left hope of return. The ant at last met one of his companions, who was also carrying a burden. They stopped, took counsel for an instant, bringing their antennæ together, and started for the hillock. The second ant then left his burden, and both together then seized a twig and introduced its end beneath the first load which had been abandoned because of its weight. By acting on the free extremity of the twig they were able to use it exactly as a lever, and succeeded almost without trouble in passing their booty on to the other side of the little hillock. It seems to me that these ants who invented the lever are worthy of admiration, and that their ingenuity does not yield to our own.

I will, finally, give an example of the methods of surmounting a difficulty of another order in utilising captured prey. It is not enough to capture prey, or even to possess the means of utilising the prey when captured. It is sometimes also necessary to prevent the booty being taken possession of by some other member of the same species as the hunter. Spiders are specially liable to this danger, because their victims are noisy when caught. Hudson has described an ingenious device made use of by a species of *Pholcus* —a quiet inoffensive Spider found in Buenos Ayres— to escape this risk. This spider, though large, is a weak creature, and possesses little venom to despatch a fly quickly. The task of killing it is therefore long and laborious, and the loud outcries of the victim may be heard for a long time, sometimes for ten or twelve minutes. The other spiders in the vicinity are naturally excited by this noise, and hurry out from their webs to the scene of conflict, and the strongest or most daring sometimes succeeds in carrying away the fly from its rightful captor. Where, however, a large colony have been long in undisturbed possession of a ceiling, when one has caught a fly he rapidly throws a covering of web over it, cuts it away, and drops it down to hang suspended by a line at a distance of two or three feet from the ceiling. The other spiders arrive on the scene, but not finding the cause of the disturbance retire to their own webs again. When the coast is thus clear, our spider proceeds to draw up the captive fly, now exhausted by its struggles.[1]

*War and brigandage.*—When Man attacks animals of another species, either to kill them and feed on their flesh, or to steal the provisions which they have amassed for themselves or their young, this is called "hunting," and is considered as perfectly legitimate. When men turn to beings of their own species either to kill them or to rob them, several different cases are distinguished. If the assailants are few in number, it is called "brigandage," and is altogether reprehensible; but if both assailant and assailed are considerable in number, the action is called "war," and receives no reprobation.

There are hunters among animals as well as among ourselves, and we have seen their various methods of procedure; but there are also brigands and warriors, and our superiority even in this department is not so absolute as might be imagined.

Independently of ordinary brigandage, which is a brutal and simple form of the struggle for life, manifested every time the animals find themselves before a single repast, there are interesting facts to be noted

[1] W. H. Hudson, *Naturalist in La Plata*, 1892, p. 189.

concerning robbers who act in a manner that Man himself would not disavow. It is worthy of remark that it is the most sociable animals who furnish us with the most characteristic examples.

Bees have a just renown as honest and laborious insects; there are, however, some who depart from the right road, and they do not do it by halves.[1] Among Hymenoptera the lazy profess the theory that pollen belongs to all bees, and that stored-up honey does not constitute private property. Therefore, to protest against work and economy, sly methods are employed by a few to utilise as their own private property the resources which Nature has made for all; they adopt the plan of plundering the working insects, and carrying away for themselves the pollen which the others had had the audacity to seek among the flowers.

To arrive at these ends these clever Hymenoptera employ cunning, and endeavour to pose as workers. They place themselves at the approaches to a hive, and when a worker arrives laden with its burden they advance towards it, caress it with their antennæ, take possession of its pollen as if to relieve it of a burden, and then fly away to their own hive.

Others adopt less diplomatic proceedings. Some unite to intrude in a badly-guarded hive, and gorge themselves with the honey to which they have no right. Following up this success, they bring accomplices; a veritable band of brigands is organised, who have no other industry than to seize honey already manufactured in order to fill their own cells. Their audacious enterprises are not always crowned with success; they are repulsed in populous and well-

[1] L. Büchner, *Aus d. Geistesleben d. Thiere*, Berlin, 1879.

organised hives, but they are successful in the weaker ones. Sometimes they act with violence, and to reduce a swarm they first fall on the queen and kill her with their stings. Disconcerted by her death, the bees allow the pillage of their dwelling, and the cells are robbed from top to bottom. In some cases the deprived proprietors, in their turn carried away by this insanity of rapine, even go over themselves to the assailing party, and carry their own honey to the house of the bandits. Henceforth they unite their fortune to that of the others, and share in their easy and adventurous life.[1]

Bates has given a vivid description of the armies of the South American Foraging Ants (*Eciton*). They are carnivorous hunters who march in large armies, and are found on the banks of the Amazon, especially in the open campos of Santarem. The *Eciton legionis* chiefly carry off the mangled larvæ and pupæ of other ants. They will attack the nests of a bulky species of the genus *Formica;* they lift out the bodies of these ants and tear them in pieces, as they are too large for a single *Eciton* to carry off, a number of carriers seizing each fragment. They seem to divide into parties, one party excavating and the other carrying away the grains of earth to a distance from the hole just sufficient to prevent them rolling back into it. There is, however, no rigid distribution of labour, the miners sometimes becoming carriers, and then again assuming the office of carrying off the prey. In marching off they form a broad and compact column, sixty or seventy yards in length, those who may be empty-

[1] P. Huber, *Recherches sur les Mœurs des Fourmis indigènes*, Paris and Genève, 1810, chap. ix.

handed assisting heavily-laden comrades. The *Eciton drepanophora* attacks and carries off all kinds of insects, especially wingless species, such as maggots, caterpillars, larvæ of cockroaches, etc. An eyeless species,[1] the *Eciton erratica*, rapidly forms covered passages under which to advance, and shows great skill in fitting the keystone to these convex arcades.[2]

Belt has also made some extremely interesting observations on the *Ecitons*, whom for intelligence he places first among the ants of Central America, and as such at the head of the Articulata.[3]

*Expeditions to acquire slaves.*—In order to reduce one's own species to slavery, it seems at first that an intelligence is required as developed as that of Man. It is necessary in fact to attack beings nearly equally well endowed from an intellectual and physical point of view. The enterprise evidently presents every possible difficulty; but in case of success, the result more than compensates for the effort. The master in future need not trouble to work, for he possesses a tool capable of doing everything as well as himself, since by means of language he can easily impress his will on the acts of the other; a domestic animal is only an auxiliary, the slave entirely replaces his owner in every labour.

Several species of ants thus obtain slaves. The best known of these is the *Polyergus rufescens.* We shall see in another chapter in what way they take advantage of slaves, and what relations they have with

1 Belt points out that blindness is an advantage in the particular mode of hunting adopted by these ants, enabling them to keep together. Those species of *Eciton* which hunt singly have very well developed eyes.

2 Bates, *Naturalist on the Amazons* (edition of 1892), pp. 355-363.

3 See *Naturalist in Nicaragua*, 1888, pp. 17-29.

them. At present it is only necessary to say how the slaves are obtained. The expeditions organised for this purpose are simply a perfected chase, both by the way in which they are conducted, and by the result to which they are to lead. It is not a question of brutally seizing a prey to be devoured immediately. The captured animal must be carefully managed, carried away alive and in such a condition that it has not yet known a free life, and can accustom itself to new conditions. When the *Polyergus* or Amazon ants desire to increase their band of slaves, one first remarks extreme excitement in the neighbourhood of the nest. They all come out helter-skelter, but this disorder lasts only for a short time; they soon form in line, and a regular serried column is formed, longer or shorter according to the swarm; it has been found to measure more than five metres long by fifteen centimetres broad. The Amazons advance, often changing their direction like a dog who is seeking a scent: this is exactly what they are doing they smell the ground with their antennæ in order to recognise traces of the *Formica fusca.* In this march the eminently republican instinct of the ants comes out. The band has no chief; those who are at the head go forward smelling the ground; this slackens their pace, so that they are passed by those in the ranks behind. Little by little they fall into single file, and this continuing during the whole course of the march, a particular ant may sometimes be at the head of the column, sometimes in the middle, sometimes in the rear. At the end of a longer or shorter period the expedition discovers a scent, which it follows up to the nest of the *Formica fusca.* The alarm is immediately given in the threatened ant-hill;

the approach is announced of a band of slavers, and they all rush out, some to face their terrible adversaries while the others take up the nymphs and eggs in their mandibles and flee in all directions to save as many as possible of their offspring. The small ants endeavour with their burdens to climb to the summits of blades of grass; those who succeed are in safety with the eggs that they carry, for the Amazons do not climb. In the meanwhile a fierce battle is going on in the neighbourhood of the nest between the *Formica fusca*, who have made a sortie, and the slavers. It is an unequal struggle, because the latter are armed with formidable jaws, strong and sharp, borne by a large head with powerful muscles. The defenders of the nest are seized and placed *hors de combat*. They flee discouraged, and the assailants force the entry of the dwelling. They then take possession of the larvæ and nymphs and come out again holding them in their mandibles. The *Polyergus* thus laden flee as fast as possible, escaping as well as they can from the bereaved parents, who endeavour to save their offspring. The band returns to the nest by the same road that it came, although not the shortest, for these insects seem to lack the sense of direction and are guided by smell, so that they have to retrace all the windings of the road. The march is slackened by the weight of the booty (Fig. 7), and each travels according to his fancy, without following the regular order of the departure. At last the ants regain their household. The slaves, warned of the return of the victorious army, rush out to meet it and relieve the arrivals of their burdens, some in their zeal even carrying at the same time both the master and his burden. The nymphs transported into the ant-hill are henceforth cared for by their fellow-slaves; the *Polyergus* do not trouble themselves further.

*Wars of the ants.*—As sociable as man, the manners of ants present more than one resemblance to his. Slave-hunting expeditions are among these; the wars that these insects undertake also resemble human wars. The causes of the quarrel are of various

FIG. 7.

nature, most often they result from the close proximity of two ant swarms. The rival colonies are always meeting in the same regions and seeking the same material; their mutual rivalry strains their relations. A moment comes when one of them is decidedly in the way of the other. At such a period, which is almost a diplomatic crisis, great excitement is observed in the two camps; there is a continual coming and going. One fine day, as the result of some unknown act,—some mysterious *casus belli* or declaration of war,—two armies place themselves on the march against each other. They advance in serried ranks. All ants do not follow the same tactics; some throw themselves out in a thicker line,

FIG. 8.

while others form in squares. But as soon as action commences the individual regains his rights. It is a series of duels, of fierce hand-to-hand struggles. Legs are torn away, heads are cut off by strokes of the jaws, abdomens are disembowelled; a terrible fury animates the combatants, and nothing will disturb them from the battle. (Fig. 8.) By-

and-by victory remains with the fiercest or the strongest; the vanquished draw in, carrying away as far as possible their wounded and their dead. Nothing more is seen on the field of carnage but separated limbs or heads which strew the ground like a multitude of small black points. Often the enmity is not extinguished after a battle, and several defeats are necessary before the weaker swarm is destroyed or forced to emigrate.[1]

[1] P. Huber, *Mœurs des Fourmis indigènes*, chap. ix. Many of the chief observations—given in the words of the original observers—as well as a summary of the facts known regarding the social activities of ants generally, will be found in the useful volume by Romanes in the International Scientific Series, *Animal Intelligence*, 1882.

# CHAPTER III.

## METHODS OF DEFENCE.

FLIGHT—FEINT—RESISTANCE IN COMMON BY SOCIAL ANIMALS—SENTINELS.

STUDYING the animal kingdom in the manner here adopted, that is to say by passing in review the various manifestations of zoological life, we are necessarily led to find certain industries which are opposed to others. We have seen the various methods of hunting; but attack calls forth defence. In the struggle for life we find the action of beings on other beings, and the re-action of these latter; the final result is the expression of the difference between the two according as one or the other is stronger.

*Flight.*—Just as the most rudimentary method of attack is simple pursuit, so the most simple and natural method of defence is flight; but if very fleet animals like hares, gazelles, and deer can escape by simply exerting their maximum rapidity, it is not always thus, and certain species exercise in flight perfected methods appropriate to circumstances, and so raise this method of defence to an art.

Of all animals the Ape most skilfully directs his flight. There is no question that in his intelligence we may find every rudiment of our own; but of all his qualities none more nearly approximates him to us than his courage. There are no animals, not even the great beasts of prey, who are so brave as Man and the Ape, and who are capable of so much presence of mind. It is perhaps this bravery which, joined to his sociability, has most contributed to assure the supremacy of the one. As to the other, the road has been barred to him by his better-endowed cousin; he is disappearing before Man, and not before nature or other animals. In thinly-inhabited regions he is still the king. It is generally considered that the Lion is the incarnation of courage, but he is the strongest and the best armed; there is none before whom he need tremble. In captivity he allows himself to be struck by the tamer, which the most miserable ape would never suffer. The Lion will struggle with extreme energy without calculating the difference of strength between his opponent and himself, and will resist as long as he is able to move. The Ape directs all his courage and presence of mind to order his flight when he has recognised a danger that is insurmountable. He does not act like those infatuated beasts who lose their head and rush away trembling, in their precipitation paralysing a great part of their resources. A band of apes in flight utilises all obstacles that can be interposed between themselves and the pursuer; they retire without excessive haste and take advantage of the first shelter met with; a female never abandons her young, and if a young one remains behind, and is in danger of being taken, the old males of the troop go back boldly to save it at the peril of their lives. In this connection many heroic facts have been narrated. This animal has too frequently been judged by comparison with ourselves;

he has been regarded as a human caricature and covered with ridicule. We obtain a very much higher idea of him if we compare him with other animals. Always and everywhere there has been a prejudiced insistance on his defects; we perceive them so easily because they are an exaggeration of our own; but he also possesses qualities of the first order.

As an example of flight arranged with intelligence, we have already seen how the *Formica fusca* profits by the difficulty experienced by the *Polyergus* in climbing. It hastily gains the summit of a blade of grass, to place there in safety the larvæ which the others wish to carry away. The ruses adopted in flight are as varied as those of attack. Every animal tries to profit as much as possible by all his resources.

Larks, a feeble race of birds, rise higher in the air than any rapacious bird, and this is often a cause of safety. Their greatest enemy is the Hobby (*Hypotriorchis sublutes*). They fear him greatly, so that as soon as one appears singing ceases, and each suddenly closes his wings, falls to the earth and hides against the soil. But some have mounted so high to pour out their clear song that they cannot hope to reach the earth before being seized. Then, knowing that the bird of prey is to be feared when he occupies a more elevated position from which he can throw himself on them, they endeavour to remain always above him. They mount higher and higher. The enemy seeks to pass them, but they mount still, until at last the Hobby, heavier, and little accustomed to this rarefied air, grows tired and gives up the pursuit.[1]

[1] *Naturgeschichte der Vögel Deutchslands*, etc.

The Gold-winged Woodpecker of the United States (*Colaptes auratus*) often escapes Falcons either by throwing himself into the first hole that he finds, or if he cannot find one, through seizing the trunk of a tree with his claws. As he is a very good climber, he describes rapid spirals around it, and the falcon cannot in flying trace such small circles. By this method the *Colaptes* usually escapes.[1]

The Fox, who is so ingenious in hunting, is not less so when his own safety is concerned. He knows when it is best to flee or to remain; he is suspicious in a surprising degree, not only of man but also of the engines which man prepares against him. He recognises them or smells them. Certain facts almost lead us to suspect that he understands their mechanism. When one of them has been surprised in his hole, and the trap has been placed before every opening, he will not emerge from the burrow. If hunger becomes too imperious, he recognises that patience will only change the manner of his death, and then he decides to dare fate; but previously he had done everything to flee without passing over the snare. As long as he had claws and strength he hollowed out the earth to form a new issue, but hunger rapidly exhausted his vigour and he was not able to complete the work. Foxes thus trapped have recognised immediately when one of these engines went off, either owing to another animal being caught or from some other reason. In this case the captive understands very well that the mechanism has produced its effect, that it is no longer to be dreaded, and he boldly emerges.

[1] Audubon, *Ornithological Biography*, New York and Edinburgh, 1831-49.

It has happened that foxes have been caught in a trap by a paw or else by the tail, when delicately endeavouring to extract the bait. Recognising the manner in which they are retained prisoners, certain of them have had the intelligence and the courage to cut off with their teeth the part engaged in the trap, and to escape thus mutilated. St. John knew a fox who thus escaped by amputating a paw, and who was able to earn his living for three or four years subsequently, when he was finally caught.

In Australia great kangaroo hunts are organised. Generally the capture is sufficiently easy, and the dogs are able to seize the kangaroo, but sometimes he makes a long and rather original defence. If possible, he directs his flight towards a river. If he reaches it he enters, and, thanks to his great height, he is able to go on foot to a depth where the dogs are obliged to swim. Arrived there, he plants himself on his two posterior legs and his tail, and, up to his shoulders in the water, awaits the arrival of the pack. With his anterior paws he seizes by the head the first dog who approaches him, and, as he is more solidly balanced than his assailant, he holds the dog's nose beneath the water as long as he can. Unless a second dog speedily comes to the rescue the first is inevitably drowned. If a companion arrives to free him, he is so disturbed by this unexpected bath that he regains the bank as quickly as possible, and has no further desire to attack this suffocating prey. A strong and courageous old male can thus hold his own against twenty or thirty dogs, drowning some and frightening others, and the hunter is obliged to intervene and put an end to this energetic defence by a bullet.[1]

[1] J. Gould, *The Mammals of Australia*, London, 1845-60.

*Feint.*—Many animals, when they cannot escape danger by flight, seek safety by various feints. The device of feigning death is especially widespread.

Many coleopterous insects and Spiders simulate death to perfection, although it has been ascertained that they do not always adopt the attitude which members of their species fall into when really dead. But they remain perfectly motionless; neither leg nor antenna stirs. McCook, who has devoted such loving study to Spiders, remarks in his magnificent work, that the Orbweavers, especially, possess this habit. "One who touches an Orbweaver when hanging upon its web will often be surprised to see it suddenly cast itself from the snare, or appear to drop from it, as though shot off by some unseen force. Unless he understands the nature of the creature he will be utterly at a loss to know what has become of it. In truth it has simply dropped upon the ground by a long thread which had been instantaneously emitted, and had maintained the Aranead in its remarkable exit, so that its fall was not only harmless, but its return to the web assured. The legs are drawn up around the body, and to the inexperienced eye it has the external semblance of death. In this condition it may be handled, it may be turned over, it may be picked up, and, for a little while at least, will retain its death-like appearance." Preyer, who has studied this phenomenon in various animals, comes to the conclusion that it is usually due to unconsciousness as the result of fright.[1] McCook is unable to accept this theory of kataplexy, so far as Spiders are concerned. "I have frequently watched

[1] *Sammlung physiologischer Abhandlungen*, Zweite Reihe, Erster Heft, 1878.

Spiders in this condition," he observes, "to determine the point in question, and their behaviour always impressed me as being a genuine feigning of death, and therefore entirely within their volition. The evidence is of such indefinite nature that one can hardly venture to give it visible expression, but my conviction is none the less decided. I may say, however, that my observations indicate that the Spiders remained in this condition as long as there seemed to be any threatened danger; now and again the legs would be relaxed slightly, as though the creature were about getting ready to resume its normal condition, but at the slightest alarm withheld its purpose and relapsed into rigidity. The slight unclasping of the legs, the faint quivering indications of a purpose to come to life, and then the instant suppression of the purpose, were so many evidences that the power of volition was retained, and that the Aranead might have at once recovered if it had been disposed to do so. Again, I think that I have never noticed anything like that gradual emergence from the kataplectic condition which one would naturally expect if the act were not a voluntary one. On the contrary, the spider invariably recovered, immediately sprang upon its legs, and hoisted itself to its snare, or ran vigorously away among the grasses."[1]

Among fish, the Perch and the Sturgeon feign

[1] H. C. McCook, *American Spiders* (1889, etc.), vol. ii. pp. 437-445. Romanes has an interesting discussion of the habit of feigning death among animals, and cautiously reaches the conclusion that it is very largely due, not to kataplexy, but to intelligent action.—*Mental Evolution in Animals*, pp. 303-316. And for some remarks on this subject by Darwin in his Essay on Instinct, see the same volume, pp. 365, 366. Also Alix, *Esprit de nos Bêtes*, 1890, pp. 543-548.

death; according to Couch,[1] the Landrail, the Sky-lark, the Corncrake adopt the same device. Among mammals, the best-known example is probably the Opossum.

An Opossum (*Didelphys azaræ*) of South America enters farms to devastate the poultry yards. When he is discovered he runs away, but is soon caught, and blows from sticks rain upon him. Seeing that he cannot escape correction he seeks at least to save his life. Letting his head fall and straightening his inert legs he receives the blows without flinching. Often he is considered dead, and abandoned. The cunning little beast, who desires nothing better, arises, shakes himself, and rather bruised, but at all events alive, takes his way back to the wood.

The Argentine Fox (*Canis azaræ*), when caught in a trap or run down by dogs, though it fights savagely at first, after a time drops down and apparently dies. "When in this condition of feigning death," Mr. W. H. Hudson remarks, "I am quite sure that the animal does not altogether lose consciousness. It is exceedingly difficult to discover any evidence of life in the opossum, but when one withdraws a little way from the feigning fox, and watches him very attentively, a slight opening of the eye may be detected; and, finally, when left to himself, he does not recover and start up like an animal that has been stunned, but slowly and cautiously raises his head first, and only gets up when his foes are at a safe distance. Yet I have seen *guachos*, who are very cruel to animals, practise the most barbarous experiments on a captive fox without being able to rouse it into exhibiting any sign of life. This has greatly puzzled

[1] *Illustrations of Instinct*, 1847.

me, since, if death-feigning is simply a cunning habit, the animal could not suffer itself to be mutilated without wincing. I can only believe that the fox, though not insensible, as its behaviour on being left to itself appears to prove, yet has its body thrown by extreme terror into that benumbed condition which simulates death, and during which it is unable to feel the tortures practised on it. The swoon sometimes actually takes place before the animal has been touched, and even when the exciting cause is at a considerable distance."[1]

It is probably a measure of prudence which impels certain birds to imitate successively the cries of neighbouring animals, in order to persuade their enemies that all the beasts in creation are brought together in this spot except themselves. It is perhaps going a little too far to suppose so reflective and diplomatic a motive, but it is not doubtful that in certain cases this custom can be very useful to them by putting their enemies on the wrong scent. In North America nearly all the species of the Cassique family have this custom. If they wish to deceive the ears of the great Falcons who watch them—or is it simple amusement?—they interrupt their own song to introduce the most varied melodies. If a sheep bleats, the bird immediately replies to the bleating; the clucking of a turkey, the cackling of a goose, the cry of the toucan are noted and faithfully reproduced. Then the Cassique returns to his own special refrain, to abandon it anew on the first opportunity.[2]

Not only do animals thus feign death in order to secure their own safety, but the female sometimes

[1] W. H. Hudson, *Naturalist in La Plata*, p. 203.

[2] Waterton, *Wanderings in South America* (First Journey), ch. iii.

endeavours to attract an enemy's attention and feigns to be wounded in order to decoy him away from her young. This trick is adopted especially by birds. In illustration of this it will be sufficient to quote from Bendire's *Life Histories of North American Birds* some observations by Mr. Ernest Thompson of Toronto, regarding the Canadian Ruffled Grouse (*Bonasa umbellus togata*), commonly called the Partridge by Canadians :—" Every field man must be acquainted with the simulation of lameness, by which many birds decoy or try to decoy intruders from their nests. This is an invariable device of the Partridge, and I have no doubt that it is quite successful with the natural foes of the bird; indeed it is often so with Man. A dog, as I have often seen, is certain to be misled and duped, and there is little doubt that a mink, skunk, racoon, fox, coyote, or wolf would fare no better. Imagine the effects of the bird's tactics on a prowling fox: he has scented her as she sits; he is almost upon her, but she has been watching him, and suddenly, with a loud whirr,' she springs up and tumbles a few yards before him. The suddenness and noise with which the bird appears cause the fox to be totally carried away; he forgets all his former experience, he never thinks of the eggs, his mind is filled with the thought of the wounded bird almost within his reach; a few more bounds and his meal will be secured. So he springs and springs, and very nearly catches her, and in his excitement he is led on, and away, till finally the bird flies off, leaving him a quarter of a mile or more from the nest.

"If instead of eggs the Partridge has chicks, she does not await the coming of the enemy, but runs to meet and mislead him ere yet he is in the neighbourhood of the brood ; she then leads him far away, and returning by a circuitous route, gathers her young together again by her clucking. When surprised she utters a well-known danger-signal, a peculiar whine, whereupon the young ones hide under logs and among grass. Many persons say they will each seize a leaf in their beaks and then turn over on their backs. I have never found any support for this idea, although I have often seen one of the little creatures crawl under a dead leaf."[1]

*Resistance in common by social animals.*—If neither flight nor feint has saved an animal from the hunter, he naturally fights as long as he can, but this struggle *in extremis* is rarely crowned with success. Certain species, especially those which live in society, are able nevertheless, by uniting their efforts, to resist enemies who would easily triumph over them if they were isolated.

Among tribes of Apes mutual assistance, as described by Brehm, is common. When by chance a bird of prey, such as an eagle, has thrown himself on a young ape who is amusing himself far from the maternal eye, the little one does not let himself be taken without resistance ; he clings to the branches and utters shrill and despairing cries. His appeals are heard, and in an instant a dozen agile males arrive to save him ; they throw themselves on the imprudent ravisher and seize him, one by the claw, another by the neck, another by a wing, pulling him about and harassing him. The bird struggles as well as he can, distributing around him blows from talons

[1] Bendire, *Life Histories of North American Birds* (*Smithsonian Contributions to Knowledge*, vol. xxviii.), 1892, p. 64.

and beak. But he is often strangled, and when his temerity does not receive this extreme punishment, the feathers which fall from him when he flies away bear witness that he has not emerged unscathed from the scuffle.

Animals like Buffaloes resist by a common defence the most terrible Carnivora. Even the Tiger is their victim, although if one of them met that wild beast alone he would surely become its prey. Being very agile, the tiger can reach by one leap the back of the ruminant, whose brutal and massive force cannot thus be exercised; but the feline who falls into the midst of a troop fares very badly. One buffalo falls on him with lowered horns, and with a robust blow of the head throws him into the air. The tiger cannot regain his senses, for as soon as he reaches the ground, and often even before, he is again seized and thrown towards other horns. Thus thrown from one to another like a ball, he is promptly put to death.

The less terrible Carnivora give Buffaloes no trouble. Wolves do not dare to attack them when they are united; they await in ambush the passage of some strayed calf, and rapidly gain possession of it before the rest of the flock are aware, or they would dearly pay for their attack.

The Bisons of North America, near relatives of the Buffaloes, also repulse Wolves in common; and if Man succeeds better against them it is owing to the skill which he shows in hiding himself and not attracting their attention. Every one knows how Indians hunt the Bison with arrows, and his pursuit is very risky to the hunter, for he must not be discovered by the game, as he would then be trodden underfoot or disembowelled. In the immense prairies where these ruminants feed, a few Indians covered by bisons' skins advance on all fours, so that nothing betrays their presence. The victims fall one by one beneath silent blows, and their companions, who can see nothing suspicious in the neighbourhood, are not disturbed, supposing them, no doubt, to be peacefully resting.

It is not only against other animals that these great mammals have to defend themselves; they are much afraid of heat, and they are accustomed, especially in the south of Persia, to ruminate while lying in the water during the hot hours of the day. They only allow the end of the snout, or at most the head, to appear. It is a curious spectacle when fording a river to see emerge from the reeds the great heads and calm eyes of the Buffaloes, who follow with astonishment all the movements of the horsemen, although nothing will disturb their sweet and fresh siesta.

But let us return to defences arranged in common. Horses are extremely sociable, and in the immense pampas of South America those who become wild again live in large troops. In difficult circumstances they help one another. If a great danger threatens them all the colts and mares assemble together, and the stallions form a circle round the group, ready to drive back the assailant. But they do not accomplish this manœuvre in the presence of an enemy of small importance. When a wolf appears on the plain all the males run after him, seeking to strike him with their feet and kill him, unless prompt flight delivers him from their blows.

The sociable humour of these horses makes them

compassionate towards their fellows who are enslaved by man, and if a harnessed cart meets on its road a free band, it is a serious matter to the owner. They run up and surround the enslaved horse, saluting him with their cries and gambols, having the air of inviting him to throw his harness to the winds and follow them on the plain, where grass grows for all without work. Naturally the driver endeavours to preserve his noble conquest, and distributes blows with the whip to those who wish to debauch it. Then the wild horses become furious, and throw themselves on the vehicle; they break it with their feet and cut their comrade's traces with their teeth to enable him to share their own free life. The enterprise satisfactorily concluded, they gallop away neighing in triumph.

It is owing to their union in large bands that Crows have so little to fear from diurnal birds of prey; if one approaches, they do not hesitate to throw themselves on him altogether. The Great Horn Owl, however, causes many ravages among them; for when asleep at night the Crow is without defence against the ravisher, for whom, on the contrary, obscurity is propitious. Thus they recognise him as a hereditary enemy, and never allow an opportunity of revenge to pass without profiting by it. If by chance an owl appears by day and one of them perceives him, immediately a clamour arises—a veritable cry of war; all those who are in the neighbourhood fly to the spot, and business ceases; the nocturnal bird of prey is assaulted, riddled with blows from beaks, stunned, his feathers torn out, and, notwithstanding his defence, he succumbs to numbers.

In all the preceding examples the social species unite for the common security the forces and effects which they can derive from their own organs.

I have spoken of the Apes and described how they defend themselves with their hands and teeth; but in certain cases they use weapons, employing foreign objects like a club or like projectiles.

Acts of this nature are considered to indicate a high degree of development, and it has often been repeated that they are the appanage of man alone; we have, however, seen the *Toxotes*, who, like all fishes, is not particularly intelligent, squirt water on to his victims. It is not easy to understand how a greater intellectual effort is required to throw a stone with the hand than to project water with the mouth. This is what the apes do, throwing on their assailants from the heights of trees everything which comes to hand: cocoa-nuts, hard fruits, fragments of wood, etc.

Baboons (*Cynocephali*) who usually live in the midst of rocks protect their retreat by rolling very heavy blocks on to their aggressors, or by forcibly throwing stones about the size of the fist. As these bands may contain from a hundred to one hundred and fifty individuals, it is a veritable hail of stones of all sizes which they roll down from the heights of the mountains where they find shelter.

*Sentinels.*—Not only do Apes know how to face danger or to avoid it by a prudent flight, but they also seek to foresee it, and to avoid exposing themselves to it. A troop of Apes, according to Brehm, generally places the leadership in the hands of a robust and experienced male. This primitive royalty is founded partly on the confidence inspired by an old chief, and partly by the fear inspired by his muscular arms and ferocious canine teeth. (Fig. 9.) He gives himself a great deal of trouble for the security of his subjects, and does not abuse the authority which he possesses. Always at the head, he leaps from branch to branch, and the band follows him. From time to time he scales a tall tree, and from its heights scrutinises the neighbourhood. If he discovers nothing suspicious a particular guttural grunt gives information to his companions. If, on the contrary, he perceives some danger he warns them by another cry, and all draw in ready to follow him in his retreat, which he directs in the same way as he guided the forward march.

Apes are not alone in relying on the experience of one of their members. Many other animals act in the same way: antelopes, gazelles, elephants, who advance in troops always conducted by an old male or female who knows all the forest paths, all the places favourable to pasture, and all the regions which must be avoided.

Others, more democratic, instead of giving up the care of their safety to one individual, which cannot be done without abdicating some degree of individual independence, dispose around the place which they occupy a certain number of sentinels charged to watch over the common safety. This custom exists among prairie dogs, mufflons, crows, paroquets, and a great many other animals. The sentinels of the crows are not only always on the watch, but they are extremely discriminating; they do not give a warning at the wrong time. It is certain that these birds can distinguish a man armed with a gun from another who merely carries a stick, and they allow the

FIG. 9.

second to approach much nearer than the first before giving the alarm.

Paroquets of all species live in joyous and noisy bands. After having passed the night on the same tree they disperse in the neighbourhood, not without having first posted watchers here and there, and they are very attentive to their cries and indications.

The great Aras or Macaws, the large and handsome parrots of the Andes, act with much prudence when circumstances make it advisable, and they know when they ought to be on their guard. When they are in the depths of the forest, their own domain, they gather fruits in the midst of a deafening noise; each one squalls and cries according to his own humour. But if they have resolved to pillage a field of maize, as experience has taught them that these joyous manifestations would then be unseasonable and would not fail to attract the furious proprietor, they consummate the robbery in perfect silence. Sentinels are placed on the neighbouring trees. To the first warning a low cry responds; on the second, announcing a nearer danger, all the band fly away with vociferations which need no longer be restrained. The common Crane (*Grus cinerea*), still more far-seeing to avoid a possible future danger, despatches scouts who are thus distinct from sentinels who inform their fellows of present danger.[1]

When these birds have been disturbed in any spot, they never return without great precautions. Before arriving, they stop; a few only go circumspectly forward, examining everything, and coming back to make their report. If this is not satisfactory the troop remains suspicious, sending new messengers.

[1] E. Poppig, *Fragmenta zoologica itineris Chilensis*, 1829-30.

When they are at last assured that there is really nothing to fear, the rest follow.

Thus by the most varied methods animals endeavour to save their threatened lives, and succeed to some extent in attaining safety. Destruction and the chase on one side, conservation and flight on the other: these are the two chief acts which occupy living beings. Many, however, less threatened, succeed in perfecting their manner of life, and employ their industry in less pressing occupations than eating others or preventing others from eating them.

# CHAPTER IV.

## PROVISIONS AND DOMESTIC ANIMALS.

PROVISIONS LAID UP FOR A SHORT PERIOD—PROVISIONS LAID UP FOR A LONG PERIOD—ANIMALS WHO CONSTRUCT BARNS—PHYSIOLOGICAL RESERVES—STAGES BETWEEN PHYSIOLOGICAL RESERVES AND PROVISIONS—ANIMALS WHO SUBMIT FOOD TO SPECIAL TREATMENT IN ORDER TO FACILITATE TRANSPORT—CARE BESTOWED ON HARVESTED PROVISIONS—AGRICULTURAL ANTS—GARDENING ANTS—DOMESTIC ANIMALS OF ANTS—DEGREES OF CIVILISATION IN THE SAME SPECIES OF ANTS—APHIS-PENS AND PADDOCKS—SLAVERY AMONG ANTS.

THE industries of the chase which are derived immediately from the most imperious of needs—that of assuring the existence of the individual—never arrive at a very extraordinary degree of perfection; or at all events, as they are indispensable to existence, we are not surprised at their development. It is unquestionable that an industry marks a higher degree of civilisation not only by its development, but still more by its reference to the less necessary things of life; in every species the importance of the place given to the superfluous is a mark of superiority. The animals who, foreseeing a hard season, or fearing the days when hunting will not be productive, lay up provisions to utilise in such times of famine, rise a degree higher than even the most skilful hunters. Not all amass with the same sagacity, and we shall find different examples of foresight, from the most rudimentary to the highest, very near what we may observe in Man.

The provisions harvested by animals have more than one destination: some are for the individual himself who has gathered them; others, on the contrary, are to serve as the food for his young at the age when they are not yet capable of seeking their own food. I will deal with these latter in another chapter, and propose at present only to speak of those animals who provision barns with the intention of themselves profiting by them.

The foresight of the animal is so much the greater the more remote the future for which he prepares. The Carnivora live from day to day and lay up no stores; it is the Rodents, certain frugivorous birds, and insects who exhibit the most complicated acts of economy.

*Provisions laid up for a short period.*—As a rudimentary example of the art of preserving food in view of possible famine, I may mention the case of the *Lanius collurio.* I have already spoken of this bird and of his custom in days of abundance of spitting on thorns all the captures he has made. One may see side by side Coleoptera, crickets, grasshoppers, frogs, and small birds. It is evident that these reserves cannot be preserved for more than a day, or at most two days. The bird amasses just enough to show us his apprehensions of the possible future lack of success in hunting, and his thought of preserving the surplus of the present in view of privations to come.[1]

The Fox, a very skilful hunter, has no trouble in finding game; of all the Carnivora he is, however, the only one who is truly foreseeing. The others in presence of abundant food gorge themselves, and abandon the rest at the risk of suffering to-morrow. The fox is not so careless. If he has had the good fortune to discover a poultry yard, well supplied but ill watched, he carries away as many fowls as he can before dawn and hides them in the neighbourhood of his burrow. He places each by itself, one at the foot of a hedge, another beneath a bush, a third in a hole rapidly hollowed out and closed up again. It is said that he thus scatters his treasures to avoid the risk of losing all at one stroke, although this prudence complicates his task when he needs to utilise his provisions. The fox, however, loses nothing, and knows very well where to find his stores. The very nature of the game prevents him from keeping it more than a few days.

*Provisions laid up for a long period.*—The Rodents, who live on dry fruits or grains, can on the other hand preserve them for a long time in their barns. The Squirrel, who may be seen all the summer leaping like a little madman from branch to branch, and who seems to have no cares except to exhibit his red fleece and show off his tail, is, contrary to appearance, a most sensible and methodical animal. He knows that winter is a hard time for poor beasts, and that fruits are then rare or hidden beneath the snow; in the autumn, therefore, when all the riches of the earth are abundant, and beech-nuts, acorns, and chestnuts

[1] Naumann, *Naturgeschichte der Vögel Deutschlands*, etc.

have ripened, he harvests quantities of them and hides them wherever he can. Making use of the cavities he is acquainted with around his domain, hollow trees, holes that he makes in the earth beneath bushes, etc., he fills them with fruits, and when winter has come he extracts them to munch.

*Animals who construct barns.*—The Field Rat of Hungary and Asia (*Psammomys*) gathers wheat during the summer. He cuts the blades and transports them to his home, where he stores them up in very considerable quantities; and during rigorous winters when famine appears also among men, gleaners of another species appear on the scene and seek for corn under the earth in the nests of the *Psammomys.* A single rat can store up more than a bushel. Those who are skilful in finding their holes can thus in a day glean a good harvest, to the detriment of the rats who are thus in their turn reduced to beggary.

The Hamster also makes provision of grain, but he introduces two improvements: the first at the harvest by only taking the edible part of the ear, and the second by constructing barns distinct from his home. Each possesses a burrow composed of a sleeping chamber, around which he has hollowed one or two others communicating with the first by passages, and intended to serve as barns. The old and more experienced animals prepare even four or five of these storehouses. The end of summer is their season for work. They scatter themselves in the fields of barley or wheat, pull down the stalks of the cereals with their anterior paws, and then cut off the ear with their teeth. This done, they set about thrashing their wheat—that is to say, they separate the grain from the straw by turning the ear round and round between their paws. When the grains come out they pile them up in their cheeks, and thus transport them to one of the chambers already mentioned; they then return to exploit the field and continue these labours until they have completed the stores for winter.

A certain Vole (*Arvicola economus*) acts in much the same way as the Hamster, though he harvests a different class of objects. It is not wheat which he collects but roots. He has to find these roots, to dig them up, to cut them into fragments of suitable dimensions for transport, and finally to pile them up in rooms disposed to receive them. This species, which inhabits Siberia, measures about twelve centimetres in length, but during summer and autumn Voles accomplish an amount of work which is surprising having regard to their size. The moment having arrived to think about winter, the Voles spread themselves about the steppe. Each hollows little pits around the roots he wishes to extract. After having bared them he cleans them while still in position, so as not to encumber his storehouses with useless earth. This preparatory labour having been completed, he divides the root into slices of a weight proportioned to his strength, and carries away the fragments one by one. Seizing each with his teeth, he walks backwards drawing it after him, and thus traverses a long road, crossing paths, going round tufts of grass or other obstacles, not letting himself be rebuffed by the difficulty and length of the task. Arrived at his hole, he enters this also backwards, drawing his burden through all his galleries. His dwelling, though the entrance is rather more complicated, resembles that of the Hamster. Like the latter, it is composed of a central room placed in communication with the outside by a maze of passages, which cross one another. That is the sleeping-room, the walls of which are well formed, and which is carpeted with hay. From this various underground passages start which lead to the storerooms, which are three or four in number. It is to these that the Vole bears his harvest. Each compartment is large enough to contain four or five kilogrammes of roots, so that the little rodent finds himself at the end of the season the proprietor of about fifteen kilogrammes of food in reserve. He would have enough to enable him to revel in abundance if he were able to reckon without his neighbours. This diligent animal has in fact one terrible parasite. This is Man, who will not allow him to enjoy in peace the fruits of his long labour and economy. In Siberia, a long and severe winter follows a very hot summer; in this season the inhabitants often lack provisions. A moment comes when they are glad to make up for want of bread by edible roots; but the search for these is long and troublesome, and should indeed have been thought of during summer. Man, during the fine weather less foreseeing than the rodent, does not hesitate when famine has come to turn to him for help. As he is the weaker, the Vole is obliged to submit to this vexatious tax. According to Pallas,[1] the inhabitants seek these nests full of provisions and dig them up. The conqueror takes all he pleases, and abandons the rest to the unfortunate little beast, who, whether he likes it or not, has to be content. In this region the

1 Pallas, *Ueber d. am Volgastrome bemerkten Wanderungen der grossen Wassermäuse* (*Arvicola amphibius*), *Nord-Beitr.*, vol. i., 1781, p. 335.

burrows of the Vole abound; therefore this singular tithe ensures a considerable revenue to those who levy it, as may be understood when we remember the extent of the stores amassed by the animal.

A Vole resembling the *Arvicola arvalis*, but larger, paler, and more rat-like, with large shining eyes and very short tail, overran in 1892-93 the classic land of Thessaly, the land of Olympus, and the Vale of Tempe. It has always inhabited this region, and the old Greeks had an Apollo Smintheus, or Myoktonos, the Mouse-destroying God. "At the beginning of March," according to Prof. Loeffler, who has given an account of this invasion,[1] "the Voles were only beginning to troop from the slopes of the hills and the fallow-lands to the cultivated fields. It was frequently observed that they followed regular paths during their inroads. Thus they advanced along the railway embankment. Their progress seemed to be rather slow. Perhaps they do not advance further till the inhabitants of one of their strongholds or so-called castles have become too numerous. The runs which they excavate are at a depth of about twenty to thirty centimetres below the surface of the ground. The extent of their runs varies, and we found them extending in length from thirty to forty metres and more. These runs are connected with the surface by vertical holes of about five centimetres in diameter. In many places four, five, and more holes have led to the same run. In such cases there is generally, not far off, an enlargement for the nest, lined with finely-ground vegetable material, where the young are pro-

[1] *Centralblatt f. Bak. u. Parasitenkunde*, July 1892, and *Zoologist*, September 1892.

duced and reared. In front of newly-opened holes the earth, which has been thrown far out, forms smooth hillocks. There were many well-defined and well-trodden paths on the ground, by which the Voles pass from one hole to another. They are never seen out of their holes by day, not even in places where the entire ground is riddled with holes like a sieve. They do not come out in search of food till the evening; even then not many are to be seen, but the peculiar squeaking noise they make is to be heard everywhere. Next day all sorts of freshly-severed plants are to be found in the holes. Stalks of corn they manipulate by standing on their hind legs and gnawing through the stalk; when this is bitten off they drag it into their holes to devour it there, sometimes making it smaller. They do their work with amazing rapidity. One evening a field was visited which was to be mowed next day, but when the labourers came in the morning they found nothing to cut. The Voles had destroyed the entire crop in a single night. A miller in the neighbourhood of Velestino reported that he went to his field early one morning, cut a measure of corn, loaded it on his ass, and brought it to his mill. When he returned to his mill with a second load he found scarcely a vestige of the first remaining. Thinking it had been stolen he kept watch for the thief; but suddenly, to his great astonishment, hosts of Voles appeared and set to work to carry off the second load." Such facts as these recorded by Loeffler are by no means a merely recent phenomenon; Aristotle was familiar with the devastations of the Voles, and wrote that "some small farmers, having one day observed that their corn was ready for harvest, when they went the following day to cut their corn, found it all eaten." Other ancient writers record similar facts.[1]

Two birds of North America, belonging to the Woodpecker family, prepare their provisions for the bad season with consummate art; not only do they harvest them and place them in shelter, but they arrange them in such a manner that at the right moment they can utilise them in the most convenient manner.

One of them which is common in California, the *Melanerpes formicivorus*, nourishes himself, as his name indicates, by insects, and especially ants. All the summer he gives himself up to this hunt, but at the same time he collects acorns, which he does not touch, however, so long as he can find other food. He amasses them in the following ingenious manner: he chooses a tree and hollows out in its trunk a cavity just capable of receiving one acorn. He then carries a fruit and introduces it forcibly into the hole he has just made. Thus buried, the acorn can neither fall nor become the prey of another animal. In the domain of these birds trees may be found which are riddled like a sieve with holes stopped up by an acorn as by a plug. When the hunting of insects ceases to be fruitful, the *Melanerpes* visits his barns. If an ordinary bird wished to eat one of these fruits, at each stroke of his beak, on account of the polish and convexity of the acorn's surface, it would escape

[1] *Zoologist*, May 1893. It may be added that the Scottish Vole, which was so destructive about the same time, does not burrow to a depth like the Thessaly Vole, but lives in shallow runs amongst the roots of herbage. Its exploits are recorded in a Report on the Plague of Field-Mice in Scotland, made by a committee appointed by the President of the Board of Agriculture, 1893.

him, and only by a series of reiterated efforts would the interior be exposed; but for the American woodpecker the task is simplified; each acorn being maintained firmly in the bark, it is sufficient to break the envelope and the pulp is easily seized.[1]

A relation of this bird, the *Colaptes mexicanus*, does not yield to him in economy and skill. He places his barn in the interior of a plant which is very abundant in the zone he inhabits. Insectivorous during a part of the year, he is forced to renounce this diet during the dry season. In the regions of Mexico where this bird is found the dry period is so absolute that he would die of hunger for want of insects or fruits if he had not taken the precaution of laying up stores during spring. His store consists of acorns. He has not time to fix them one by one, like the *Melanerpes*, and only thinks at first of rapidly collecting a large quantity. But it is in deciding the question as to where they are to be laid up that the *Colaptes* shows his remarkable intelligence. In the forests where he lives are to be found aloes, yuccas, and agaves. When the agaves have flowered, the flower-bearing stem, two or three metres in length, shrivels, but remains standing for some time. Its peripheral portion is hardened by the heat, while the sap in the interior almost entirely disappears. A hollow cylinder with a well-sheltered cavity is thus formed, and the *Colaptes* proposes to utilise it as a storehouse. His acorns will there be well protected against external influences and against the birds whose beaks are too weak to pierce the agave. It is then a question of filling

[1] See, for instance, *Nature*, 20th July 1871; also A. L. Heermann, "Notes on the Birds of California," *Journ. Acad. Nat. Sc. Philadelphia*, 2nd Series, vol. ii., 1853, p. 259.

the tube. The animal first pierces the wall towards the base of the stalk; through this hole he introduces acorns until he has filled the lower part of the cavity. This done, he makes a new hole rather above the first, and fills the interval between the two, continuing this process until he has arrived at the top of the stalk and filled the whole interior. (Figs. 10 and 11.) The bird seems at first to take unnecessary trouble by boring so many holes. He would reach his end as well, it would seem, by making a single hole at the top to fill his storehouse, and another at the bottom to empty it. But we must not thus accuse him of lack of judgment. The interior of the tube is just large enough for the passage of an acorn; but at certain points the sap is not entirely absorbed, and there might easily be an impediment which would leave a large part of the cavity empty. Hence the necessity for a number of openings. When the sun has scorched up plants, and provisions are rare, he turns to his barns of abundance. Now and every time that he has need he can utilise the method that has been employed by his cousin the *Melanerpes*. In order to feed on each acorn without too much trouble, or allowing it to slip from his beak, the bird places it in a vice. He hollows a hole in the trunk of a tree, introduces the fruit there forcibly, and eats it at his ease.[1]

The provisions collected by these two birds reveal a remarkable fact. They possess indeed two distinct diets; they do not preserve for the period of famine the overplus of the foods which they consume in the period of abundance. They chase insects and feed on

[1] Henri de Saussure, "Observations sur les mœurs de divers oiseaux du Mexique," *Arch. Sci. phys. et natur.*, 1859, pp. 21-41.

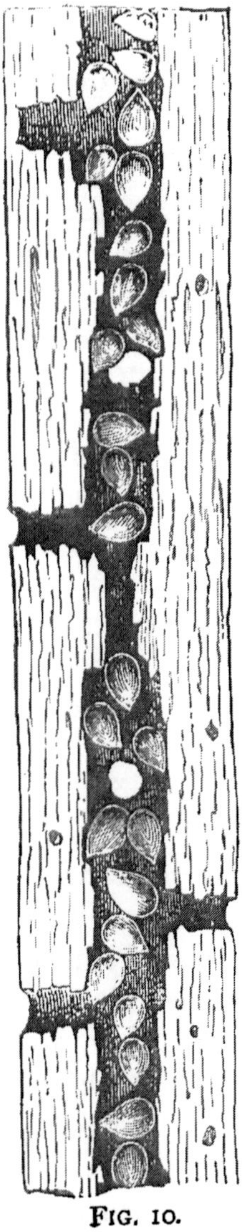

FIG. 10.

FIG. 11.

them as long as they can find them, while they gather up in their storehouses an entirely different food.

*Physiological reserves.*—All the animals of which I have just spoken place their provisions for the future in barns in the same manner as Man. Those who have not this foresight are either able to nourish themselves in all seasons by the chase, or else, after having feasted one half of the year, they fast during the other half. In the latter case they consume during the fasting period a portion of their own substance, and use up materials placed in reserve in their organism, in the form of fat for example. This arrangement, which allows them to prolong life, though growing thin, until the next season of prosperity, is not under the control of the will. It is a complication of physiological phenomena resulting from the functioning of different parts of the organism.

*Stages between physiological reserves and provisions.*—Between physiological reserves and industrial stores we may place as an intermediate stage the interesting case of the Honey Ants.[1]

These insects (*Myrmecocystus*) live in Texas, and form colonies in which certain individuals play a very special part. They exaggerate to an extreme point the power of preserving provisions in their crops. These materials are not assimilated; they do not form part of the animal's body, and although placed inside it cannot be compared to physiological reserves. It is especially curious that they are not to be utilised only by the animal itself, but also by the other members of the colony who are not able to form

[1] H. C. McCook, *The Honey Ants of the Garden of the Gods, and the Ants of the American Plains*, Philadelphia, 1882.

such stores. Among the *Myrmecocystus* there are workers of two sorts; the first kind resemble other ants with some differences of detail, and build and hollow the earth nest which shelters the community. The second kind is quite different; the abdomen in these workers is enormously distended so as to constitute a voluminous sphere, which may become four or five times larger than the thorax and head together. (Fig. 12.) On this distended receptacle appear several darker plates; these are the remains of the chitinous parts of the primitive wings. In the fine season these ants go out in a band and collect a sweet liquor which forms pearly drops on certain galls of oak leaves. These drops, elaborated into honey, gradually fill the crop, distending it and pushing back neighbouring organs until it receives its globular form. When they have arrived at this obese condition, the heavy honey ants no longer leave the nest. They remain without movement, hanging by their legs to the roof or lying against the walls of a room. The workers who have remained slender come and go, attending to their usual occupations, and pass near the others without paying attention to them or going out of the way to lend assistance to their impotent sisters when one of them has rolled over on the ground and can no longer arise unaided. (Fig. 13.) They only cease to be indifferent when impelled by the selfish sentiment of hunger, and then it is to ask and not to give assistance. The fat ants in

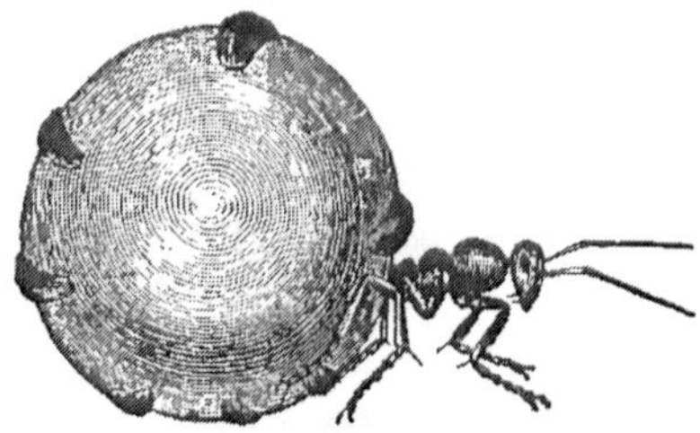

FIG. 12.

fact could not themselves consume all the honey that they have elaborated; the others in times of famine approach them, caress them with their antennæ, and obtain by solicitation a drop of honey which the large ones disgorge from the crop. Here, then, is a colony in which the division of labour has reached a remark-

FIG. 13.

able degree of polymorphism. Some of the members accomplish the work of engineers and masons, while the others fabricate for the community a store of honey. Instead of depositing these provisions in cells like bees, they preserve them in their own digestive tube. This custom has re-acted to such an extent on the form of their bodies that at first sight they seem to belong to a different species.

*Animals who submit foods to special preparation in order to facilitate transport.*—Not content with collecting materials as they are found in nature, certain animals submit them to preparation with various aims, either to render transport easier or that they may not deteriorate when stored. Among those of whom I have just spoken, some collect with the view of utilising their stores in a more remote future than others. The *Ateucus sacer* intends to consume the provisions he prepares almost immediately. Yet he acts in so careful a manner that I cannot pass him in silence. This beetle is the sacred Scarabæus so venerated by the Egyptians, who have everywhere reproduced his image in porphyry and granite. He is a most singular insect. The celebrated Fabre has given a complete and very picturesque history of his customs.[1] I have myself had an opportunity of seeing him at work. It was in Persia, in the plain of Susiana, on a hot morning in March. We had passed the night in the open air, proposing to continue our journey in the early morning, but our mules, rendered rather lively by the fresh grass brought out by the spring weather, had decided otherwise. They had all decamped to take a ramble on their own account. In order to pass away the hours taken up by the mulateers in searching for the strayed animals, the Scarabæus would, I thought, furnish me with an amusing and instructive spectacle. During the night the mules had not failed to leave here and there the relics of their digestion. The aroma, borne on the morning breeze, had struck the Scarabæus on awak-

[1] J. H. Fabre, *Souvenirs entomologiques*, 1879.

ing. It was his favourite dish. From all points of the sky their heavy silhouettes could be seen against the blue. It was still fresh, the sun having only risen about an hour before; the heat would soon become oppressive, and the sybaritic beetle, without attending to his morning appetite, which his fresh meal could not fail to excite, nourishes the bourgeois dream of making his little pile in order to enjoy himself sheltered from the hot rays. Immediately on arriving on the scene of the accident each began to display feverish activity. All set to work.

FIG. 14.

With their heads, the anterior edge of which is flat and supplied with six strong spines, they raised their provisions; with their anterior feet, which are large and also armed with spines, they moulded the paste and placed it beneath the abdomen between the four other legs, giving it a rounded form. Little by little the sphere increased and acquired the size of a small apple. That was sufficiently large, and besides it was already becoming hot. The insect set about carting away his prize to a sheltered dining-room.

He placed his four posterior legs on the ball; with the two last, which were continually moving, he made certain of the equilibrium of the mass; then resting his head and two anterior feet on the ground he pushed backwards, and with extreme rapidity. (Fig. 14.) There was enough for all; each worker could find the just reward for his labour; I witnessed none of the regrettable facts narrated by Fabre. It happens sometimes, according to this ingenious observer, that a cunning Scarabæus, who has taken no part in the laborious labour of moulding the paste, arrives when it is on the road to aid the convoy, or even simply to pretend to help, in order that when the moment has come he may claim a share in the coveted meal, or even carry it all away if he can profit by a momentary inattention on the part of the lawful proprietor. I followed one of these Coleoptera for more than five metres from the place where his labour began. After having deposited his ball he began to dig up the earth around it;[1] but the mules had returned and I was obliged to depart.

I have no doubt that subsequent events were not exactly the same as narrated by Fabre for the Scarabæus of Provence. The insect having made his hole, buries himself in it for a *tête à tête* with the precious sphere. He immediately sets about passing the whole through his body. Without haste but without rest, for a week or a fortnight, as long as there is any of it left, he eats continuously, and continuously digests. He does not stop for a moment, his jaws are working the whole time; and Fabre has called attention to the fact that

[1] In captivity also, as Mrs. Brightwen found, the Scarabæus always attempts to bury its ball in the earth.

from the opposite extremity of the animal a continuous thread emerges without breaking, and becomes coiled up.

*Care bestowed on harvested provisions.*—Among the animals who take particular care of the provisions they have amassed, special mention must be made of certain species of Ants. It was formerly believed that these industrious Hymenoptera are not accustomed to store up in barns for the winter. This opinion long prevailed owing to the authority of Huber, so competent in these matters, although the ancients were well acquainted with the storehouses of ants.[1] But it was founded on an exclusive study of these insects in northern countries, in which, during the cold season, they become torpid and buried in their hybernal sleep. Naturally they have no need of food during this period, but it was incorrect to generalise from this fact. The ants of the south are active all the year round. An English naturalist, Moggridge, who passed several winters at Mentone, has placed this fact out of doubt. Suffering from an incurable disease, he occupied the last years of his life in observing and setting down for the instruction of others the habits of these insects. He found that ants of the species *Atta barbara* store up grains. They utilise plants of various kinds, but usually fumitory, oats, nettle, various species of *Veronica*, etc. They procure these grains towards the end of autumn, collecting them on the soil, or even, when they do not fall in sufficient quantities, climbing up the plants and gathering them in position. An ant will, for instance, ascend the stem of a fruiting plant, of shepherd's-purse, let us say, and select a

1 See chapter on "The Ancient Belief in Harvesting Ants," in McCook's *Agricultural Ants.*

well-filled but green pod, mid-way up the stem, those below being ready to shed their seeds at a touch. Then seizing it in its jaws, and fixing its hind legs firmly as a pivot, it contrives to turn round and round, and so to strain the fibres of the fruit-stalk until they snap; it then patiently backs down the stem. Sometimes two ants combine their efforts; one, at the base of the peduncle, gnaws at the point of greatest tension, while the other hauls upon it and twists it. And sometimes the ants drop the capsules to their companions below, corresponding with the curious account given by Ælian of the way the spikelets of corn are thrown down "to the people below." In this labour they display the activity usual in their race, and do not stop until they have carried away to their barns the amount of provision they desire. When their wealth is stored up in the nest, the ants pile up the grains in some hundred little rooms designed for this purpose, each measuring from seven to eight centimetres in diameter, and three or four in height; the average granary being about the size of a gentleman's gold watch. Adding up the quantities of grain divided between these different barns, it is found that they may be estimated at about 500 or 600 grammes, which represents a very large number of meals for such small appetites, and must cost colossal labour if we take into consideration the size of the workers. But when the harvest is completed, the *Atta barbara* have not completed their task; they are too ingenious to limit themselves to waiting with crossed legs for the moment to come when they may enjoy their labour, without considering the damage that may arise. Their first care is to prevent the grains from germinating for some weeks. How they obtain this result is not exactly known, but it is certain that germination does not take place, although all the conditions of heat and moisture offered by the interior of the ant-hill are favourable to it; it is not less certain that this arrest is due to the ants. This is shown in a very simple manner. It is sufficient to prevent the access of the insects to one of these chambers to cause the grains to germinate immediately. We can only suppose some direct action of the ants, every other hypothesis falling before this single fact: the arrested phenomenon is produced as soon as the *Atta barbara* no longer acts on it. Therefore they arrest germination without rendering it impossible, and when the moment arrives for utilising the accumulated stores, their first care is to allow the grains to follow the normal course of evolution. The envelope breaks, the little plant makes its appearance; radicle and stalk come to light. But the ants do not permit the development to go too far. The little plant, in order to grow, digests the starch which is associated with the albumen, for it is not yet able to draw its nourishment direct from the soil. To be absorbed and assimilated this starch must first be transformed into sugar. This chemical transformation being effected, the grain is in the condition in which the ants prefer it. Like a wine-grower who watches over the fermentation in his vat, and stops it before the wine turns sour, they stop the digestion of the starch at this stage. If we do not know how they retard germination, we know at all events how they render it impossible at this later stage. It is the young plant which absorbs the glucose, and which must therefore be destroyed; they cut off the radicle with their mandibles, and gnaw the stalk; the germ is thus suppressed. They have not yet finished their manipulations, which must enable them to preserve without further alteration the provisions which they have already rendered palatable. They bring out all their provisions to the sun, dry them, and take them back to the barns. As long as winter lasts they feed on this sweet flour. An anatomical peculiarity enables them to make the most of it; their mouth is so arranged that they can absorb solid particles and eat the albuminous powder. In this they differ from their northern kin, who are obliged to feed exclusively on juices.

I have compared the labours of these ants to those of the wine-grower. Both of them in fact utilise the chemical phenomena going on in living matter; both of them know how at a given moment to prevent the transformation from going further. Neither of them for the rest take into account the part played by diastasis and ferments. The ancestors of one as of the other have by chance found out the method, and they transmit it from generation to generation.[1]

*Agricultural Ants.*—The art of amassing stores is still more highly perfected by an Ant which inhabits North America. It is called the *Pogonomyrmex barbatus*, or, on account of its customs, the Agricultural Ant. It carries out a certain number of preparatory acts, and pushes foresight further than any other animal, since it looks after its property while still growing. It is grain which these insects collect, but only a single species of graminaceous grain. This choice leads them to spend great trouble

[1] J. Treherne Moggridge, *Harvesting Ants and Trap-Door Spiders*, London, 1873, pp. 16-60.

on their preferred plant. They act in such a way that in the case of men we should say, purely and simply, that they were cultivating. The art of treating the earth with a view of augmenting the products which it yields is certainly of all the manifestations of human activity that which we should least expect to find among animals. It is, however, impossible otherwise to describe the conduct of Agricultural Ants. The field which they prepare is found in front of their ant-hill; it is a terrace in extent about a square metre or more; there they will allow no other plant to grow but that from which they propose to gather fruit. This latter (*Aristida stricta*) is rather like a grain of oats, and in taste resembles rice; in America it is called ant rice. This culture represents for these insects a much more important property than a wheat field for man. It is, in relation to their size, a forest planted with great trees, in comparison with which baobabs and sequoias are dwarfs. It is not known if the *Pogonomyrmex* sow their rice; Lincecum asserted that the ants actually sow the seeds, that he had seen the process going on year after year; "there can be no doubt," he concludes, "of the fact that this particular species of grass is intentionally planted, and in farmer-like manner carefully divested of all other grasses and weeds during the time of its growth."[1] McCook is not able to accept this unqualified conclusion. "I do not believe that the ants deliberately sow a crop, as Lincecum asserts, but that they have, for some reason,

[1] Lincecum's most important published paper on the habits of the *Myrmica mollefaciens* appeared in the *Proc. Acad. Nat. Sci. Philadelphia*, vol. xviii., 1866, p. 323-331. See also Darwin, *Proceedings of the Linnæan Soc.*, 1861.

found it to their advantage to permit the *Aristida* to grow upon their disks, while they clear off all other herbage; that the crop is seeded yearly in a natural way by droppings from the plant, or by seeds cast out by the ants, or dropped by them; that the probable reason for protecting the *Aristida* is the greater convenience of harvesting the seed; but, finally, that there is nothing unreasonable, nor beyond the probable capacity of the emmet intellect, in the supposition that the crop is actually sown. Simply, it is the Scotch verdict—Not proven."[1] However it may be, they certainly allow no other plant to grow in the neighbourhood of their grain, to withdraw the nourishment which they wish to reserve entirely for it. Properly speaking, they weed their field, cutting off with their jaws all the troublesome plants which appear above the soil. They pursue this labour very diligently, and no strange shoot escapes their investigations. Thus cared for, their culture flourishes, and at the epoch of maturity the grains are collected one by one and carried within. Like all harvesters, these Hymenoptera are at the mercy of a shower that may fall during the harvest. They are well aware that in this case their provisions would be damaged, and that they would run the risk of germination or decay in the barns. Therefore, on the first sunny day all the ants, as observed by Lincecum and Buckley, may be seen carrying their grains outside, only bringing them back when they have been thoroughly dried, and always leaving behind those that have sprouted.[2]

[1] H. C. McCook, *Natural History of the Agricultural Ants of Texas*, Philadelphia, 1879, pp. 33-39.

[2] McCook, *Agricultural Ants of Texas*, pp. 105-107.

*Gardening Ants.*—The Leaf-cutting Ants (*Œcodoma*) of tropical America are often alluded to by travellers on account of their ravages on vegetation; and they are capable of destroying whole plantations of orange, mango, and lemon trees. They climb the tree, station themselves on the edge of a leaf and make a circular incision with their scissor-like jaws; the piece of leaf, about the size of a sixpence, held vertically between the jaws, is then borne off to the formicarium. This consists of low wide mounds, in the neighbourhood of which no vegetation is allowed, probably in order that the ventilation of the underground galleries may not be interfered with.

For a long time there was considerable doubt as to the use to which the leaf-cutting ants put the leaves; some naturalists supposed they are used directly as food, others that the ants roof their underground dwellings with them. The question was set at rest by Fritz Müller, who observed these ants in Brazil,[1] and independently by Belt, who studied them in Nicaragua, and has written an interesting account of their proceedings.[2] The real use of the leaves is as manure on which to grow a minute species of fungus; these ants are, in reality, mushroom growers and eaters. Belt several times exposed the underground chambers to observation and found that they were always about three parts filled with "a speckled, brown, flocculent, spongy-looking mass of a light and loosely-connected substance." Scattered throughout these masses were the pupæ and larvæ, together with the smallest division of workers who do not engage in leaf-carrying, but whose duties appear to be to cut up the

[1] *Nature*, 11th June 1874. And see Appendix.

[2] *Naturalist in Nicaragua*, 2nd edition, 1888, pp. 71-84.

leaves into small fragments and to care for the young. On examination the masses proved to be composed of "minutely sub-divided pieces of leaves, withered to a brown colour, and overgrown and lightly connected together by a minute white fungus that ramified in every direction throughout it." That they do not eat the leaves themselves was shown by the fact that near the tenanted chambers were found deserted ones filled with the refuse of leaves that had been exhausted as manure, and which served as food for the larvæ of various beetles. There are numerous holes leading up from the underground chambers, and these are opened out or closed up, apparently in order to regulate the temperature below. Great care is also taken that the nest should be neither too dry nor too damp; if a sudden shower comes on the leaves are left near the entrance, and carried down when nearly dry; during very hot weather, on the other hand, when the leaves would be parched in a very short time, the ants only work in the cool of the day and during the night. Occasionally, inexperienced ants carry in grass and unsuitable leaves; these are invariably brought out again and thrown away.[1]

*Domestic animals of Ants.*—Following through different species the perfection reached in the art of laying up provisions for the future, we have gradually arrived at methods resembling those of Man. But a foresight still greater and nearer to his is manifested by those ants who breed and keep near them animals of different species, not for the sake of their flesh, but for certain secretions, just as man utilises the milk

[1] For a brief discussion of the relation of ants to plants generally, see Lubbock's *Ants, Bees, and Wasps*, 1882, chap. iii.

of the cow or the goat. Ants have true domestic animals belonging to a variety of species, but the most widely spread are the *Claviger* and the Aphides or plant-lice. To keep these insects at their disposal, Hymenoptera act in various ways: some, who are a little experienced, are content to take advantage of a free aphis which chance may put in their way; others shut up their cattle in stables situated in the midst of the ant-hill, or else pen them in the country at a spot where they can best find their food. These facts have long since been carefully studied and leave no room for doubt.

The *Claviger testaceus* is a small beetle, often met in the dwellings of ants. Nature has not been very generous on its behalf. It is blind, and its eyes are indeed altogether atrophied. The elytra are soldered at the median edge, so that it cannot spread its wings to fly. It is an animal predestined to the yoke; and for the rest its masters treat it with extreme kindness. The yellow ants, according to Müller,[1] have reduced this outcast beetle to domesticity, and it is almost a piece of good fortune for him to have lost his freedom and to have gained in exchange a shelter and a well-furnished trough. These insects are in fact cared for by their masters, who feed them by disgorging into their mouths the sweet liquids they have gathered here and there. If a nest is disturbed the ants hasten to carry their eggs and larvæ out of danger; they display the same solicitude with regard to the *Claviger*, and carefully bear them to the depth of their galleries. It must not be believed

[1] Ph. W. J. Müller, "Beiträge zur Naturgeschichte der Gattung *Claviger*," *Germer. u. Zincken's Magaz. d. Entomol.*, iii., 1881, pp. 69-112.

that the practical insect takes so much care in order to repair the injustice of nature towards the beetle; the part of a devoted sick nurse would not suit him; he cares for the *Claviger* because it is his property, a capital which brings in interest in the shape of excellent sweet little drops which are good to suck.[1]

A yellow ant, who wishes to enjoy the result of the cares given to his pensioner, approaches it and gently caresses it with his antennæ; the other shows signs of pleasure at this visit, and soon a pearly drop appears on the tuft of hairs at the edge of its elytra, and this the ant hastens to lick. The beetle is thus exploited and tickled by all the members of the community to which he belongs who meet him on their road. But when it has been milked two or three times it ceases to

[1] There is little doubt, however, that some species of Aphides and allied Coccidæ would be liable to extermination if not protected by their ant masters. See, for instance, Forel, *Bull. Soc. Vaud.*, 1876. Mr. Cockerell in Jamaica has noted an interesting Coccid, *Icerya rosæ*, which is protected by ants; "at the present moment some of these *Iceryæ* are enjoying life, which would certainly have perished at my hands but for the inconvenience presented by the numbers of stinging ants."—*Nature*, 27th April 1893. Mr. Romanes (*Nature*, 18th May 1893) quotes as follows from a letter addressed to him by the Rev. W. G. Proudfoot:—"On looking up I noticed that hundreds of large black ants were going up and down the tree, and then I saw the aphides. . . . But what struck me most was that the aphides showered down their excretions independently of the ants' solicitations, while at other times I noticed that an ant would approach an aphis without getting anything, and would then go to another. I was struck with this, because I remembered Mr. Darwin's inability to make the aphides yield their secretion after many experiments. A large number of hornets were flying about the tree, but seemed afraid of the ants; for when they attempted to alight, an ant would at once rush to the spot, and the hornet would get out of its way."

secrete. A solicitous ant arriving at this moment finds its efforts in vain, but still behaves like a good shepherd; it shows no impatience or anger towards its exhausted beast, knowing well that it is only necessary to come back a little later or to go to another member of the herd. Nor are his cares lessened by finding the source dried up. He foresees that it will still be good after repose, and if it is hungry he disgorges food for it.

*Degrees of civilisation in the same species of Ants.*—These facts are sufficiently marvellous in themselves, but are more surprising when we recollect that they cannot be regarded as an innate and unreflecting instinct with which all the individuals of the same species are endowed. The art of domesticating the *Claviger* is a stage of civilisation reached by some tribes and not by others. Lespès[1] has placed this out of doubt in the following manner. He had specimens of *Lasius niger* who exploited a flock of Coleoptera. Having met ants of the same species who possessed no flocks, he brought them some. At the sight of the little insects they threw themselves on them, killed them, and devoured them. If we compare these facts with those which pass in human societies, it will seem to us that these latter Hymenoptera behave like a horde of hunters in the presence of a flock of sheep, while the first have already arrived at the sheep-herding stage.

*Aphis-pens and paddocks.*—Ants can also keep Aphides in their homes. In this case, fearing that the adult beasts may not be able to adopt a change of surroundings and food, they bring the eggs to their

[1] "Recherches sur quelques Coleoptères aveugles," *Ann. Sc. Nat.*, v. Série, t. ix., 1868, p. 71.

nests and care for them at the same time as their own children. In time they come out and constitute a flock easy to tame. Other ants, still more intelligent, have discovered a method of holding the Aphides captive, while allowing them to enjoy their accustomed life, and to feed at will on the foods they prefer on their own favourite spots. It is sufficient for this purpose to establish barriers around a group of cattle who have themselves fixed the place of their sojourn. The *Lasius niger*, a skilful architect, constructs vaulted passages from his dwelling into the country. These covered roads, built with earth moistened with saliva, have various ends; some have been made in order to reach remote work sheltered from the sun, or to give concealment from enemies. Many lead to the pens of the Aphides; they reach from the ant-hill as far as the foot of a plant where these insects are abundant. In order to have their milkers at their disposal, without removing them from pasture, the ants make tunnels along the stalk, and enclose within it all the Aphides they meet. They thus prevent any desire for a distant ramble. But in order that the flock may not be too closely confined, the *Lasius niger* enlarge the galleries in places, and make a sort of chamber or stable in which the beasts may disport themselves at ease. These halls, which are proportionately very vast, are supported against the branches and leaves of the plant which bears up the walls and the vaults. The captives find themselves then with all the advantages of material life, and may be milked with every facility.[1]

An allied species of ant, the *Lasius brunneus*, lives

[1] P. Huber, *Recherches sur les Mœurs des Fourmis indigènes*, pp. 176-200.

almost entirely on the sweet secretion of large Aphides in the bark of oaks and walnut trees. The ants construct around these insects cabins made of fragments of wood, and wall them in completely so as to keep them at their own disposal.

The *Myrmica* also forms similar pasture lands; its system is rather less perfect than that of the *Lasius*, as it does not form covered galleries to reach its stables. It is content to build large earth huts around a colony. A large hole, which allows the passage of the ants, but not the escape of the flock, is formed so that they may come to milk their cows. They use the same methods we have seen practised on the *Claviger*, caressing the insect with their antennæ until the sugared drop appears.[1]

An example is quoted which shows still greater intelligence and foresight in Ants. They have been known to repopulate their territories after an epidemic, or at least after the destruction of their Aphides. The proprietor of a tree, finding it covered with these exploited beasts, cleared it of its inconvenient guests by repeated washes; but the dispossessed Hymenoptera, considering that this pasture close to their nest was very convenient for a flock, resolved to repopulate it, and for some time these tenacious insects could be seen bringing back among the foliage Aphides captured elsewhere.[2]

[1] In Central America, Belt has described how the Leaf-hoppers are milked for their honey by various species of Ants, and also by a Wasp. He considered that some species of Leaf-hopper would be exterminated if it were not for the protection they received from Ants.—*Naturalist in Nicaragua*, 1888, pp. 227-230.

[2] P. Huber, *Recherches*, etc., pp. 210-250; Lubbock, "On the Habits of Ants," *Wiltshire Arch. and Nat. Hist. Mag.*, 1879, pp. 49-62.

*Slavery among Ants.*—The custom of making slaves is widely spread in the ant world; I have already described the expeditions organised to obtain them. We will now consider the relations of these insects among themselves.

The *Formica sanguinea* takes possession of the eggs of the *Formica fusca* and rears them with its own. When the slaves reach the adult condition they live beside their masters and share their labours, for the latter work, are skilful in all tasks, and can by their own activity construct an ant-hill and keep it going. If they desire servants, it is not in order to throw all the work on them, but to have intelligent assistants. This is the primitive form of slavery as it first existed among men. It was not until later that it became modified, to become at last an institution against which the sentiment of justice arose. Other species of Ants have pushed the exploitation of slaves to a point Man has never reached. But the *Formica sanguinea* are companions to their helpers rather than masters, and even show them great consideration. When the colony emigrates one may see the owners of the nest, who are of larger size than the *Formica fusca*, take these up in their jaws and carry them the entire way.

The Amazons (*Polyergus rufescens*) act otherwise. Very skilful in obtaining slaves and powerfully armed for triumphant raids, their nests always contain legions of servants, and the custom of being waited upon has become so impressed on the race by heredity that it is an instinct stronger even than personal preservation. The master ant has not only lost the taste and the idea of work, but even the habit of feeding himself, and would die of hunger beside a pile of honey or sugar if a grey ant was not there to put it into his mouth. Thus Huber, the earliest accurate observer of these ants, enclosed thirty Amazons with several pupæ and larvæ of their own species, and twenty negro pupæ, in a glass box, the bottom of which was covered with a thick layer of earth; honey was given to them, so that, although cut off from their auxiliaries, the Amazons had both shelter and food. At first they appeared to pay some little attention to the young; this soon ceased, and they neither traced out a dwelling nor took any food; in two days one-half died of hunger, and the other remained weak and languid. Commiserating their condition, he gave them *one* of their black companions. This little creature, unassisted, formed a chamber in the earth, gathered together the larvæ, put everything into complete order, and preserved the lives of those which were about to perish.

All their industry is expended in the acquisition of captives. The *Polyergus* avoid introducing into their houses adults who would not become reconciled to the loss of liberty, and would prefer to die rather than work for others. They carry off the larvæ of *Formica fusca* and *Formica cunicularia*. When brought into the ant-hill these larvæ are placed in the jaws of slaves of their own species, who care for them; they are born captives, and have neither the regret nor the idea of a free life. Among the Amazons the slaves undertake every labour; it is they who build and who care for the larvæ of their masters, as well as those carried away in expeditions. They have also complicated personal services towards the *Polyergus*. They bring them food, lick off the dust from their hairs, clean them, carry them from one place to another, if there is need to emigrate, although they themselves are much smaller. The masters, by force of losing interest in work, lose also their votes when it is a question of taking a resolution concerning the whole colony. The servants act on their own initiative and their own responsibility, direct constructions according to their own ideas, and even in grave concerns, such as emigration, the idle masters do not seem to be consulted. The workers deliberate among themselves, and having come to a decision, proceed to execute it. They transport the household gods, the eggs, the future of the city, and the Amazons who have become its parasites. It is a most curious fact that the slaves should submit to this precarious fate when their masters are absolutely dependent on them. It is just to add that the robust mandibles of the latter may contribute to preserve the position they enjoy.[1]

[1] Lubbock has a brief discussion on the relations of Ants to their domestic animals and to their slaves, *Ants, Bees, and Wasps*, chap. iv.

# CHAPTER V.

## PROVISION FOR REARING THE YOUNG.

THE PRESERVATION OF THE INDIVIDUAL AND THE PRESERVATION OF THE SPECIES—FOODS MANUFACTURED BY THE PARENTS FOR THEIR YOUNG—SPECIES WHICH OBTAIN FOR THEIR LARVÆ FOODS MANUFACTURED BY OTHERS—CARCASSES OF ANIMALS STORED UP—PROVISION OF PARALYSED LIVING ANIMALS—THE CAUSE OF THE PARALYSIS—THE SURENESS OF INSTINCT—SIMILAR CASES IN WHICH THE SPECIFIC INSTINCT IS LESS POWERFUL AND INDIVIDUAL INITIATIVE GREATER—GENERA LESS SKILFUL IN THE ART OF PARALYSING VICTIMS.

*The preservation of the individual and the preservation of the species.*—In the previous chapter we have seen animals preparing for the future, and amassing materials for their own subsistence. In other cases these provisions are destined to feed the young. It is the same industry, sometimes exercised for the preservation of the individual, sometimes for the perpetuation of the race. We must expect to find acts of the last kind more instinctive and less reflective than those of the first, and this agrees well with what we know of natural selection. If we now see living beings display so many resources and calculate with such certainty all that will favour the healthy development of their descendants, we must not necessarily conclude that the species possess these instincts from the beginning. They are not to be regarded as mechanisms artfully wound up and functioning since the appearance of life on the earth with the same inevitable regularity. The qualities which we find in them were weak at first; they have developed in the course of ages, and have finally, by heredity, been impressed upon the creatures to manifest themselves by necessary acts from which there is no longer any escape. There is no need for surprise if we meet to-day, I do not say among all, but among a very large number of animals, this foresight for offspring in a well-marked form. It is easy to understand that the species that first acquired and fixed an instinct propitious to the increase of the race has rapidly prospered, stifling beneath its extension those that are less favoured from this point of view, which is of capital importance in a struggle for a place beneath the sun. At the present day if the struggle of animal life offers few facts of lack of foresight for the rearing of young, it is because this defect has killed the races who were subject to it; they have disappeared, or have only been saved by qualities of another order.

For the rest, if it is difficult to reconstitute except in imagination the different stages through which, in time, and in a determined species, acts at first imperfect, but designed, have become perfect and instinctive, we can at least find in space different degrees of the same instinct in allied genera which lead us by a succession of transitions from mechanical action to reflective action.

As I cannot quote all the facts showing this care for the future, I will select a few. It must be said at first that a considerable number of animals show nothing of the kind. Let us leave aside all the inferior beings to speak of those among whom we may expect some degree of method. Crustacea, fish, Batrachians, and many others lay their eggs, are contented to conceal them a little so that they may not become a too easy prey, and are altogether indifferent as to what may happen afterwards. As soon as they come out, the young obtain their own food from day to day; myriads are destroyed, and if the races remain so strong numerically it is because they are saved by the innumerable quantity of eggs produced by a single female. If it were not for this prodigious fecundity these species would have disappeared. Birds make no provision for their young; but, on the other hand, as long as the latter are weak and unable to obtain their own prey, the parents feed them every day by hunting both for themselves and the brood.

I will not insist on those beings who, like mammals, produce physiological reserves, not for their own use, but for the profit of their young. The females of these animals elaborate materials from their own organism and store them up in the form of milk to nourish the young. This fact is related to foresight, with a view to offspring, exactly in the same way as the Honey Ants show a transformation of foresight for the individual. In both cases industry is replaced by the function of a specially adapted organ.

*Foods manufactured by the parents for the young.*—It is especially insects with whose industries we are here concerned, and they are more or less instinctive in various cases. Every one knows how the Hymenoptera prepare honey from the pollen of flowers, to some extent for themselves, but especially in order that their young may at the moment of appearance possess a food which will enable them to undergo their first metamorphosis sheltered from the inclemencies outside. These foods are enclosed with great art, according to the species, either in skilfully-constructed cells of wax, as by Bees, or in nests of paper or cardboard which the Wasps fabricate, or again in huts built of earth in the manner of the *Chalicodoma.*

*Species which obtain for their larvæ foods manufactured by others.*—Other insects have not this taste for lengthy labours, and do not know how to execute them; but they do not intend that their young shall be the victims of maternal lack of skill, and they display marvellous resources to enable them to profit by the foresight of others.

The *Sitaris muralis*, a beetle whose customs have been described by Fabre in a remarkable manner,[1] may be counted among the cleverest in assuring to its larvæ the goods of others. It puts them in a position to profit by it, and when they are installed they know sufficiently well what to do. The species has so long perpetuated itself by this process that it has become, both in mother and offspring, highly automatic. It is a hymenopterous insect which this family, whose first vital manifestation is theft, thus levies a contribution on. It is called the *Anthophora pilifera*, and during the fine weather it makes a collection of honey intended to be absorbed by its

[1] "Hypermetamorphoses et Mœurs des Meloïdes," *Ann. Sc. Nat.*, iv. Série, t. 7, 1857, p. 299; also "Nouvelles observations sur l'hypermetamorphose et les Mœurs des Meloïdes," *ibid.*, t. 9, 1858, p. 265.

own larvæ, if it had not the misfortune to be watched by one of these intriguing Coleoptera. Wherever in Provence there is a perpendicular wall, natural or artificial, a little cliff, a sloping ditch, or the wall of one of those caves which the people of the country use for putting their tools in, the *Anthophora* hollows out galleries, at the bottom of which he builds a certain number of chambers. He fills each of them with honey, places in it an egg which floats in the midst of this little lake of nectar, and closes it all up. The *Sitaris* covets this honey to nourish its offspring, and the chamber to shelter it. After having discovered one of the galleries of which I have spoken, the female *Sitaris* comes about the beginning of September to lay her eggs, which are numerous, being not generally fewer than two thousand. In the following month the larvæ appear; they are black, and swarm in a little heap mixed up with the remains of egg-shells. They vegetate in this condition for a long time, and may still be found there in May. At this period they have become more active, and, in order to complete their development, are thinking of profiting by their favourable situation near the entrance to a gallery of the Hymenoptera; when a male *Anthophora* comes within reach, two or three of them catch hold of him and climb on to his thorax. They maintain themselves there by clinging to the hairs. At the moment of fertilisation the male, thus burdened, comes in contact with the female; the coleopterous larvæ then pass on to her, so that, according to Fabre's expression, the meeting of the sexes brings death and life to the eggs at the same time. Henceforth fixed on this laying insect, the little *Sitaris* remain quiet, and have only to wait; their future is assured.

The *Anthophora* has made her chambers, and with the greatest care has filled each of them with honey. Then in the midst she deposits an egg, which remains floating on the surface like a little boat; when her task is accomplished, the mother passes to a new cell to confide to it another of her descendants. During this time the parasite larva hastily descends the abdominal hairs and allows itself to fall on the egg of the *Anthophora*, to be then borne upon it as upon a raft; its fall must take place at the precise instant which will enable it to embark without falling into the honey, in which just now it would be glued fast, and perish. This series of circumstances results only in the introduction of a single *Sitaris* into a chamber; the moment which must be profited by is too short for many of them to seize. If the female *Anthophora* carries others hidden in her hairs, they are obliged to await a new hatching to let themselves glide off. Thus enclosed with the egg of the *Anthophora* and its provision of honey, the larva has no other rival to fear, and may alone utilise the whole store. This parasitism has to such an extent become a habit with the species, that the larva's organisation has become modified by it. At the moment when it falls into the cell it cannot feed on honey. It is indispensable for its development that it should first devour the egg on which it floats; it can at this period be nourished by no other food. In acting in this way it also frees itself from a voracious being who would require much food. This first repast lasts about eight days, at the end of which it undergoes a moult, takes another form, and begins to float on the honey, gradually devouring it, for at this stage it becomes able to assimilate honey. Slowly its development is completed, with extremely interesting details with which we need not now concern ourselves. The larva of *Sitaris* is then in conditions exceptionally favourable for growth; but, in spite of appearances, there is no reason for admiring the marvellous foresight and extraordinary sureness of instinct; nearly everything depends on a fortuitous circumstance, a chance. This becomes very evident if we study another related beetle; it is called the *Sitaris colletis*, and lives at the expense of the

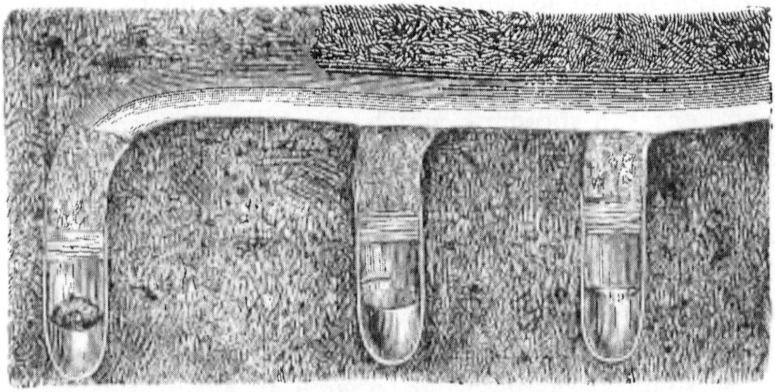

FIG. 15.

hymenopterous *Colletes*, as its relative at the expense of the *Anthophora*. But these two species of the same genus are very unequally aided by chance. The one whose history we have just traced attaches itself to an insect whose egg floats above a store of honey; the second chooses a victim who attaches its egg to the walls of a chamber. (Fig. 15.) This almost insignificant difference has a considerable influence on the parasite's evolution. In the first case it is alone, and may develop with certainty; in the second, on the contrary, several *Sitaris* penetrate the chamber and climb up to attack the egg, which in this case also must be their first food. This rivalry causes a struggle to the death. If one of the larvæ is notably more vigorous than its rivals, it may free itself from them and survive. Let us consider the fate in store for the two species. The first is much more favoured, since a happy chance permits each germ to produce an individual; in the second, each individual which completes its evolution deprives several of its brothers of life. And even this only happens in the most favourable cases, for it may be that not one *Sitaris* in the chamber may reach the adult state. If the first arrival begins to absorb the egg of the *Colletes*, a second hungry one may kill it in the midst of its repast and take its place. But the conqueror finds the provisions already reduced and insufficient to enable it to reach the moulting stage, at the end of which it could profit by the honey. Ill-nourished and weakened, it cannot support this crisis, and its corpse falls beside that of its fellow whom it had sacrificed. Three or four parasites may thus succeed to the same feast, and the victory of the last is useless to him. His first struggle for life and his first triumph are followed by irreparable defeat. These two examples show very well how a slight difference may favour a species, and how a happy quality is capable of being perpetuated by heredity, since by its very nature it is destined to be extended to more numerous beings.

*Carcasses of animals stored up.*—These insects lay up for their offspring stores manufactured by themselves or by others. The class we are now about to consider makes provision of animals either dead or in a torpid condition, with more or less art and more or less sure instinct. Most people have seen the *Necrophorus* or Burying Beetle working in fields or gardens. These are large Coleoptera who feed on abandoned carrion; everything is good to them—bodies of small mammals, birds, or frogs; they are very easy to please, and as long as the beast is dead that is all they require. When they have found such remains, and consider only how to satisfy their hunger, they do not take much trouble, and gnaw the prey on the spot where they have found it. They are not alone at the feast, and in spite of their diligence numerous rivals come up to dispute it; it is necessary to share with a great number of noisy and voracious flies and insects. In the adult state they come out well from this competition; but as good parents they wish to save their larvæ from it, as in a feeble condition these might suffer severely. They desire to lay up a carcass for their young alone, and with this object they bury it in the earth. The eggs also which will thus develop in the soil have more chance of escaping destruction by various insectivorous animals. If these diggers find a rat (Fig. 16) or a dead bird, three or four unite their efforts, glide beneath it, and dig with immense activity, kicking away with their hind legs the earth withdrawn from the hole. They do not pause, and their work soon perceptibly advances. The rat gradually sinks in the pit as it grows deeper. When they have the good fortune to find the earth soft they can sink the prey in less than two hours to a depth of thirty centimetres. At this level they stop, and throw back into the hole the earth they have dug out, carefully smoothing the hillock which covers the grave. Thus stored up, the carcass is ready to receive the *Necrophorus* eggs. The females enter the soil and lay on the buried mammal; then they retire, satisfied to leave their little ones, when they appear, face to face with such abundant nourishment. When they emerge from the envelope the young larvæ find themselves in the presence of this stored food, which has been softened by putrefaction and rendered more easy of digestion. If the treasure has not fallen on a spot easy to dig, the *Necrophorus* quickly recognise the fact, and do not waste time in useless labour. Endowed with considerable strength relatively to their size, three or four of them creep beneath the prey,

FIG. 16.

and co-ordinating their efforts they transport it several metres off to a spot which they know by experience to be suitable for their labours. It may happen that soft earth is too far away, and transport becoming too difficult a task, they renounce it. But as good food should never be wasted, they utilise it by feeding themselves, awaiting a more manageable god-send for their offspring.

Many observers have studied these beetles, and all are surprised at their sagacity, and the way in which their various operations are adapted to circumstances; genuine reflection governs their acts, which are always combined to produce a definite effect.

*Provision of paralysed living animals.*—It is unnecessary to say how much better it would be for the young larva to have at its disposal instead of a carcass a living animal, but paralysed and rendered motionless by some method. It is difficult to believe the thing possible, yet nothing is better established. There is a hymenopterous relative of the Wasp called the *Sphex.* Instead of laying up honey they store animal provisions for their larvæ. Fabre has studied one of them, the *Sphex flavipennis.*[1] It is in September that this wasp lays her eggs; during this month to shelter her little ones she hollows out a dozen burrows and provisions them. She has then to devote about three days' work to each of them, for there is much to do, as may be imagined. For each of these hiding-places the *Sphex* first pierces a horizontal gallery about two or three inches long; then she bends it obliquely so that it penetrates

[1] "Étude sur l'instinct et les metamorphoses des Sphégiens," *Ann. Sci. Nat.*, 1856.

deeply into the earth, and it is again continued in this direction for about three inches. At the end of this passage three or four chambers are made, usually three; each of these is meant to receive one egg. The insect interrupts its mining task, not forming the three chambers consecutively; when the first is completed she provisions it—we shall soon see in what manner—and lays an egg there; then she blocks it up, suppressing all communication between this cell and the gallery; this done she bores a second passage, provisions it, and lays another egg, closes up the orifice, and proceeds to prepare the third. This work is pushed on with great activity, and when completed the *Sphex* entirely fills up the subterranean passage, and completely isolates the hope of the race at a depth sufficient to shelter it well. A last precaution is taken: before leaving, the rubbish in front of the obstructed opening is cleared away, and every trace of the operation disappears. The nest is then definitely abandoned, and another one prepared.

The chambers in which the larvæ are enclosed—hastily made with little care, and with rough unsmoothed walls—are not very solid, and could not last long without slipping; but as they only have to last for a single season they possess sufficient resistance for the insect's purpose. The larva also knows very well how to protect itself against the roughness of the walls, and overlays them with a silky secretion produced by its glands.

We have now to consider the nature of the provisions placed by the *Sphex* near the egg. Each cell must contain four crickets. That is the amount of food necessary for a larva during its evolution, and these insects are in fact large enough to supply a considerable amount of nourishment. When the *Sphex* interrupts digging operations it is to fly on a hunting expedition. It soon returns with a cricket it has seized, holding it by one antenna which it turns round in its jaws. It is a heavy burden for the slender *Sphex* to bear. Sometimes on foot, dragging its burden after it, sometimes flying, and carrying the suspended cricket always in a passive condition, the burrow is gradually reached, not without difficulty. In spite of appearances, the cricket is not dead; it cannot move, but if kept for several days it will not putrefy, and its joints remain supple. It is simply the victim of a general paralysis.

*The cause of the paralysis.*—It was evidently of the greatest interest to know how the *Sphex* contrived this capture, and what method it used to suppress the movements of the prey. In order to obtain the solution of this problem, Fabre during a long period accumulated experiments and observations, and at last discovered in every detail how the thing was done. In order to compel the *Sphex* to act in his presence, he placed himself in front of the orifice of a gallery in which the insect was working; he soon saw it returning with a paralysed cricket. Arrived at the burrow, the insect placed the prey on the ground for a moment and disappeared in the passage to see that everything was in order, and that no damage had taken place since its departure. Everything was going well, and it reappeared, took up its burden, and again entered the subterranean passage, drawing the victim along. It brought it into the chamber for which it was destined, placing it on its back, the head down and the feet towards the door. Then it set out hunting again until it had ranged four crickets side by side. Before attempting a decisive experiment, the observer felt his way. At the moment when the *Sphex* was buried in the earth examining the chamber, Fabre withdrew the prey a short distance and awaited events. Having made the domiciliary visit, the *Sphex* then went straight to the place where it had left its insect, but could not find it. It was naturally very perplexed, and examined the neighbourhood with extreme agitation, not knowing what had happened, and evidently regarding the whole affair as very extraordinary; at last it found the victim it was seeking. The cricket still preserved the same immobility; its executioner seized it by an antenna and drew it anew to the entrance of the hole. In the interior of the subterranean domain everything is in good order; the insect had just assured itself of the fact, and we should expect to see it enter with its prey; not at all, it entered alone, and only decided to introduce the prey after it had made a fresh inspection. This fact is surprising, and it is still more surprising that if the practical joke of removing the cricket is repeated several times in succession, the *Sphex* drags it anew every time to the entrance of the burrow and first descends alone; forty times over this experiment succeeded without the insect deciding to renounce the habitual manœuvre. Fabre insists on this fact, and rightly, for nothing should be neglected; he makes it a text to show how automatic instinct is, and how the acts which proceed from it are invariably regulated so as to succeed one another always in the same order. In their nature these acts are quite indistinguishable from intelligent acts; only the creature is not capable of modifying them to bring them into harmony with unforeseen circumstances. All this is correct, but where it becomes excessive is in endowing animals alone with instinct and separating them from this point of view from Man. It is incontestable that the custom of visiting the burrow before introducing a victim into it has become so imperious in the *Sphex* that it cannot be broken, even when it is of no use. It is a mechanical instinct. But we may see an exactly parallel manifestation of human intelligence. In face of danger man utters cries of distress; they are heard and assistance comes. But these appeals are not intelligent and appropriate to the end; they are instinctive. Place the same individual in a situation where he knows very well that his voice cannot be heard; this will not hinder him from reproducing the same acts if he finds himself in the presence of danger. It is thus that the *Sphex* proceeds, guided by instincts, and it is no reason for despising it. And even in the course of this little experiment the insect gives proof of judgment. When it finds its cricket, it is perfectly aware that it is the same cricket which it brought, that there is no life in it, and that there is no need to re-commence the struggle; it sees too that it is not an ordinary corpse liable to putrefaction, but the very same cricket, and it does not hesitate to utilise it at once.

These habits being ascertained, Fabre proceeded to find out how the paralysis is produced. He awaited near a burrow the *Sphex's* arrival, dragging a victim by an antenna, and while the insect was occupied in the subterranean survey he substituted a living cricket for that which the *Sphex* had left, expecting to find it on the spot where it had been placed. On emerging it perceives the cricket scampering away; not a moment was to be lost, and without reflection it leapt on the refractory victim. A lively struggle followed, a duel to the death among the blades of grass; it was a truly dramatic spectacle, the agile assailant whirling around the Cricket, who kicked violently with his hind legs. If a blow were to reach the *Sphex* it would be disembowelled; but it avoids the blows skilfully without ceasing its own violent attack. At last the combat ends; the cricket is brought to earth, turned on to its back, and maintained in this position by the *Sphex*. Still on its guard, the latter seizes in its jaws one of the filaments which terminate the abdomen of the vanquished, placing its legs on the belly; with the two posterior legs it holds the head turned back so as to stretch the under side of the neck. The cricket is unable to move and the conqueror's sting wanders over the horny carapace seeking a joint, feeling for a soft place in which it can enter to give the finishing stroke. The dart at last reaches, between the head and the neck, the spot where the hard portions articulate, leaving between them a space without covering. The joint in the armour is found. The *Sphex's* abdomen is agitated convulsively; the sting penetrates the skin, piercing a ganglion situated just beneath this point; the venom spreads and acts on the nervous cells, which can no longer convey messages to the muscles. That is not all; the sting wanders over the cricket's belly, this time seeking the joint between the neck and the thorax; it finds it, and is again thrust in with fury; a second ganglion of the nervous chain is thus perforated and poisoned. After these two wounds the victim is completely paralysed.

As already mentioned, several facts enable us to recognise that the Cricket is by no means dead. It is simply incapable of movement, as would happen after an injection of curare. This poison kills a superior animal, for it hinders the muscular movements of the chest and diaphragm, necessary to respiration; but if a frog, which can breathe through its skin, is thus acted on it comes to life again at the end of twenty-four or forty-eight hours if the dose has not been too strong. The cricket is in a similar condition; it neither eats nor breathes; being incapable also of movement, there is no vital expenditure; it remains in a sort of torpor, or latent life, awaiting the tragic fate that is reserved for it. When it has been deposited in the little mortuary chamber the *Sphex* lays an egg on its thorax. The larva will soon come out to penetrate the body of the prey by enlarging the hole left by the sting. It thus finds for its first meals a food which unites the flavour of living flesh with the immobility of death. Nothing can be more convenient. When the first body is eaten it proceeds to the second, and thus devours successively the four victims stored up by maternal foresight.

In order not to interrupt the description and interfere with the succession of the acts, I have passed without remark the experiment in which Fabre substituted a living animal for the *Sphex's* already paralysed captive. It seems to me, however, that in this circumstance the insect showed judgment, and knew how to act in accordance with new requirements. It was evidently the first time in insect memory in which so surprising a phenomenon had been seen as a victim at the last moment again taking the field. We cannot make instinct intervene here. If the *Sphex's* acts are so automatic as we are sometimes led to believe, in accordance with facts which are perfectly accurate, we ought always to observe the following succession of acts: first, hollowing of the burrow; second, the chase; third, the blows of the dart; fourth, the different manœuvres for placing the victim in the sarcophagus. Now in the present case the insect had accomplished the first three series of actions, and had even begun the fourth; it ought next to drag the cricket into the burrow without listening to the recriminations which the latter had no business to make, since it was to be regarded as having received the two routine doses of poison. But the *Sphex* sees its victim come to life, understands this fact, and without seeking to fathom the cause judges that a new struggle and new blows of the sting are necessary; he understands that it is necessary to begin afresh, since the usual result has not been attained. He is then capable of reflection, and the series of acts which he accomplishes are not ordained with such inflexibility that it is impossible for him to modify them in order to conform them to varying circumstances.

The *Sphex occitanica* acts in the same manner as its relative in this complicated art of laying up provisions for the family. The differences are only in detail. Instead of hollowing the burrow first and then setting out on the chase to fill it, it does not devote itself to the labour of digging until a successful expedition has already assured the victim. (Fig. 17.) Instead of attacking crickets it seeks a larger orthopterous insect, the *Ephippigera.* The struggle is no doubt more difficult, but the result is proportionately greater, and the pursuit does not need to be so often renewed; a single captive is sufficient for its larva.[1]

FIG. 17.

*The sureness of instinct.*—It is not doubtful that a sure inherited instinct conducts the *Sphex* to prick its victim in the situation of the nervous ganglia, which will be wounded in the act. It may be said that the lesion results from the position in which the hymenopterous insect maintains its victim; for the sting is on the median line, and can only

[1] For some remarks on the action of the *Sphex*, and for Darwin's opinion on the matter, see Romanes' *Mental Evolution in Animals*, pp. 299-303.

penetrate at the soft points; the two points attacked are then rigorously determined by physical circumstances. But these arguments have no bearing if we consider the method of procedure adopted by the *Ammophila*,[1] a hymenopterous insect related to the preceding, which paralyses caterpillars. It is free in this case to insert its sting at any portion of the body; yet it knows how to turn over and arrange the captive so that the dart shall penetrate both times at two points where ganglia will be poisoned and immobility without death be induced. It must then be agreed that there is here an instinct much too sure to be called mechanical; but these facts, which considered alone seem simply marvellous, become much less so, and lend themselves to evolutionary interpretation, when it is recognised that they are related by insensible degrees to other facts of the same order, much more intelligent and at the same time less sure.

*Similar cases in which the specific instinct is less powerful and individual initiative greater.*—Here is, for instance, the case of the *Chlorion*, where each animal possesses more considerable initiative.[2] It attacks the Cockroach. These insects are of an extremely varied size, according to age, and as they are also very agile the *Chlorion* is not certain of being always able to obtain victims of the same dimension. The orifice of its burrow, which it hollows in walls between the crevices of the stones, is calculated on the average size of its victims. It has also the habit of paralysing the cockroach by

[1] Paul Marchal, "Observations sur *l'Ammophila affinis*," *Arch. de Zool. exp. et génér.*, ii. Série, t. x., 1892.

[2] Réaumur, *Memoires pour servir à l'histoire des Insectes*, Paris, 1742, t. vi., pp. 282 284.

stinging it on the nervous chain. These preliminary operations do not impede it, but it is embarrassed when it wishes to introduce through the entrance of its gallery an insect which is too large. It pulls at first as much as it can, but seeing the failure of its efforts it does not persevere in this attempt, and comes out to survey the situation. Decidedly the victim is too large and cannot pass through. The *Chlorion* begins by cutting off the elytra, which maintain it rigid and prevent it from being compressed. This done, it harnesses itself anew and re-commences its efforts. But this is not sufficient, and the victim still resists. The insect returns, and again examines the situation. Now it is a leg which is placed crossways and opposes the introduction of the body; strong diseases need strong remedies, and our *Chlorion* sets itself to amputate this encumbering appendage. It triumphs at last; the cockroach yields to its efforts, and little by little penetrates the hole. As may be seen, the labour is laborious and painful, and may present itself beneath various aspects which call for a certain ingenuity on the part of the animal.

Up to recent years the *Cerceris* was considered to act with as much certainty as the *Sphex*, and to obey an infallible instinct which always guided it for the best in the interests of its offspring. The insects it attacks belong to the genus *Buprestis*. It consumes them in considerable numbers. Its manner of action, as described by Léon Dufour,[1] much resembles that of the *Sphex*, and it would be superfluous to describe it. The only fact which I wish to mention, and

[1] "Histoire des *Cerceris*," *Ann. Sc. Nat.*, ii. Série, t. xv., 1841, pp. 353-370.

which has been put out of doubt by the illustrious naturalist, is this: the *Buprestis* are paralysed, not dead; all the joints of the antennæ and legs remain flexible and the intestines in good condition. He was able to dissect some which had been in a state of lethargy for at least a week or a fortnight, although, under normal conditions, these insects in summer decay rapidly, and after forty-eight hours cannot be used for anatomical purposes. Another observer, Paul Marchal, took up this question afresh, and the results which he obtained seemed to indicate an instinct much less firm than earlier studies tended to show.[1]

*Genera less skilful in the art of paralysing victims.*—These researches show us that in the *Cerceris* instinct is still subject to defect. In some neighbouring genera we can seize it, as it were, in process of formation. The way in which the *Bembex*, or Sand Wasp, provisions burrows by maternal foresight is much less mechanical than that of the *Sphex*. It is again Fabre who has described with most care the customs of this hymenopterous insect.[2] It hollows out for each egg a chamber communicating with the air by a gallery, and performs this work with little care and very roughly. Less skilful than the others, it does not amass at once all the provisions which its larvæ will need during the period of evolution. When the offspring has absorbed the last prey brought, it is necessary to bring a new victim. This insect is scarcely more advanced than birds, who feed their young from day to day. And it is a great labour to re-open every time the gallery which leads to the

[1] *Arch. de Zool. exp.*, 1887.

[2] *Souvenirs entomologiques*, 1879, pp. 225 *et seq.*

nursery; on all these visits, in fact, the *Bembex* fills it up on leaving, and causes the disappearance of all revealing traces. It is obliged to take so much trouble, because it has not inherited from its ancestors the receipt for the paralysing sting; it throws itself without care on its victim, delivers a few chance blows, and kills it. Necessarily it cannot, under these conditions, lay up provisions for the future; they would corrupt, and the larvæ would not be benefited; hence the obligation of frequently returning to the nest, and of a perpetual hunt to feed descendants whom nature has gifted with an excellent appetite. According to the age of the offspring, the mother chooses prey of different sizes; at first she brings small Diptera; then, when it has grown, she captures for it large blow-flies, and lastly gadflies.[1] It will be seen, then, that if we suppose the instinct of the *Sphex* to be slowly developed by being derived from a sting given at random, we make a supposition which is quite admissible and rests on ascertained facts. However this may be, the *Bembex*, returning to its burrow, is able to find it again with marvellous certainty, in spite of the care taken to hide it by removing every trace that might reveal its existence. It is guided by an extraordinary topographic instinct, which men not only do not possess, but cannot even understand the nature of.

It would appear that certain Hymenoptera, fearing to kill their victim with the sting, and not knowing

[1] A Wasp found in La Plata, the *Monedula punctata*, as described by Hudson (*Naturalist in La Plata*, pp. 162-164), is an adroit fly-catcher, and thus supplies her grub with fresh food, carefully covering the mouth of the hole with loose earth after each visit; as many as six or seven freshly-killed insects may be found for the use of one grub.

the art of skilful lesions, attempt to immobilise them by wounds of another sort. This is the case with the *Pompilius*, according to Goureau,[1] who has studied it. This insect nourishes its larvæ with spiders; it seems certain that in most cases the spider is not pricked. Victims who have been taken from the interior of provision burrows can live for a long time in spite of their wounds; they cannot, therefore, have received venom by inoculation. The author already quoted believes that the Pompilius seizes its captive by the pedicle which unites the abdomen to the cephalo-thorax, and that it triturates this point between its jaws. From this either death or temporary immobility may follow. The *Pompilius* also makes up for its relative ignorance by considerable ingenuity. Thus sometimes, when it fears a return to life of the victim destined for its larvæ, it cuts off the legs while it is still passive. Goureau has found in the nest of this insect living spiders with their legs cut off.

[1] "Observations pour servir à l'histoire de quelques Insectes," *Ann. Soc. entomol. de France*, t. 8, 1839, p. 541.

# CHAPTER VI.

## DWELLINGS.

ANIMALS NATURALLY PROVIDED WITH DWELLINGS—ANIMALS WHO INCREASE THEIR NATURAL PROTECTION BY THE ADDITION OF FOREIGN BODIES—ANIMALS WHO ESTABLISH THEIR HOME IN THE NATURAL OR ARTIFICIAL DWELLINGS OF OTHERS—CLASSIFICATION OF ARTIFICIAL SHELTERS—HOLLOWED DWELLINGS—RUDIMENTARY BURROWS — CAREFULLY-DISPOSED BURROWS — BURROWS WITH BARNS ADJOINED — DWELLINGS HOLLOWED OUT IN WOOD — WOVEN DWELLINGS—RUDIMENTS OF THIS INDUSTRY—DWELLINGS FORMED OF COARSELY-ENTANGLED MATERIALS — DWELLINGS WOVEN OF FLEXIBLE SUBSTANCES—DWELLINGS WOVEN WITH GREATER ART—THE ART OF SEWING AMONG BIRDS—MODIFICATIONS OF DWELLINGS ACCORDING TO SEASON AND CLIMATE—BUILT DWELLINGS—PAPER NESTS—GELATINE NESTS—CONSTRUCTIONS BUILT OF EARTH—SOLITARY MASONS — MASONS WORKING IN ASSOCIATION—INDIVIDUAL SKILL AND REFLECTION—DWELLINGS BUILT OF HARD MATERIALS UNITED BY MORTAR—THE DAMS OF BEAVERS.

ANIMALS construct dwellings either to protect themselves from the cold, heat, rain, and other chances of the weather, or to retire to at moments when the search for food does not compel them to be outside and exposed to the attacks of enemies. Some inhabit these refuges permanently; others only remain there during the winter; others, again, who live during the rest of the year in the open air set up dwellings to bring forth their young, or to lay their eggs and rear the offspring. Whatever the object may be for which these retreats are built, they constitute altogether various manifestations of the same industry, and I will class them, not according to the uses which they are to serve, but according to the amount of art displayed by the architect.

In this series, as in those which we have already studied, we shall find every stage from that of beings provided for by nature, and endowed with a special organ which secretes for them a shelter, up to those who are constrained by necessity to seek in their own intelligence an expedient to repair the forgetfulness of nature. These productions, so different in their origin, can only be compared from the point of view of the part they play; there are analogies between them but not the least homology.

*Animals naturally provided with dwellings.*—Nearly all the Mollusca are enveloped by a very hard calcareous case, secreted by their mantle: this shell, which is a movable house, they bear about with them and retire into at the slightest warning.

Caterpillars which are about to be transformed into chrysalides weave a cocoon, a very close dwelling in which they can go through their metamorphosis far from exterior troubles. It is an organic form of dwelling, or produced by an organ. It is not necessary to multiply examples of this kind; they are extremely numerous. In the same category must be ranged the cells issuing from the wax-glands which supply Bees with materials for their combs in which they enclose the eggs of the queen with a provision of honey.

I do not wish to insist on creations of this kind which are independent of the animal's will and reflection. Near these facts must be placed those in which animals, still using a natural secretion, yet endeavour to obtain ingenious advantages from it unknown by related species.

There is, for example, the *Macropus viridi-auratus*, or Paradise-fish, which blows air bubbles in the mucus produced from its mouth. This mucus becomes fairly resistant, and all the bubbles imprisoned and sticking side by side at last form a floor. It is beneath this floating shelter that the fish suspends its eggs for its little ones to undergo their early development.

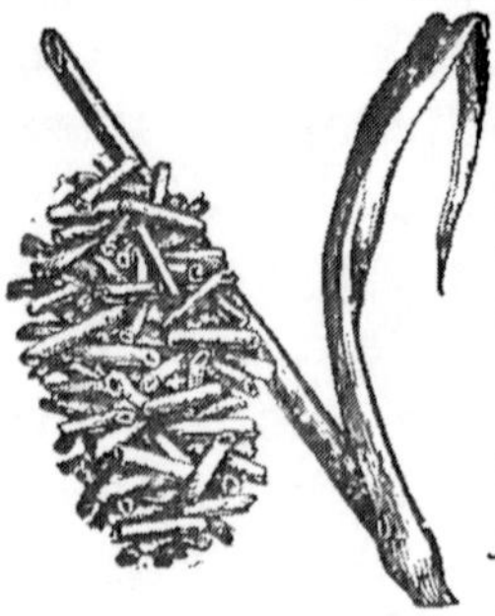

FIG. 18.

*Animals who increase their natural protection by the addition of foreign bodies.*—Certain tubicolar Annelids, whose skin furnishes abundant mucus which does not become sufficiently hard to form an efficacious protection, utilise it to weld together and unite around them neighbouring substances, grains of sand, fragments of shell, etc. They thus construct a case which both resembles formations by special organs and manufacture by the aid of foreign materials. The larvæ of *Phryganea*, who lead an aquatic life, use this method to separate themselves from the world and prepare tubes in which to dwell. (Fig. 18.) All the fragments carried down by the stream are good for their labours on condition only that they are denser than the water. They take possession of fragments of aquatic leaves, and little fragments of wood which have been sufficiently long in the water to have thoroughly imbibed it and so become heavy enough to keep themselves at the bottom, or at least to prevent them from floating to the surface. It is the larva of *Phryganea striata* which has been best studied; those of neighbouring species evidently act much in the same way, with differences only in detail. The little carpenter stops a fragment rather longer than his own body, lies on it and brings it in contact with other pieces along his own sides. He thus obtains the skeleton of a cylinder. The largest holes are filled up with detritus of all kinds. Then these materials are agglutinated by a special secretion. The larva overlays the interior of its tube with a covering of soft silk which renders the cylinder water-tight and consolidates the earlier labours. The insect is thus in possession of a safe retreat. Resembling some piece of rubbish, it completes its metamorphosis in peace, undisturbed by the carnivora of the stream. There is here already a tendency towards the dwellings of which I shall speak later on, and which are entirely formed of the external environment.

*Animals who establish their home in the natural or artificial dwellings of others.*—Between the beings whom nature has endowed with a shelter and those who construct it by their own industry, we may intercept those who, deprived of a natural asylum and not having the inclination or the power to make one, utilise the dwellings of others, either when the latter still inhabit them, or when they are empty on account of the death or departure of the owner. In the natural sciences there is no group of facts around which may be traced a clear boundary; each of them is more or less closely related to a group which appears at first of an entirely different nature. Thus it does not enter into our plan to speak of parasites. Yet, if among these some turn to a host to demand of him both food and shelter, if even they can come to be so modified and so marked by parasitism that they can live in no other way, there are others who ask for lodging only from an animal better protected than they are themselves. It is these whose customs we are called upon to consider. In the interior of the branchial chamber of many bivalvular Mollusca, and especially the Mussel, there lives a little crustaceous commensal called the Pea-crab (*Pinnoteres pisum*). He goes, comes, hunts, and retires at the least alarm within his host's shell. The mussel, as the price of its hospitality, no doubt profits by the prizes which fall to the little crab's claws. It is even said that the crab in recognition of the benefits bestowed by his indolent friend keeps him acquainted with what is passing on around, and as he is much more active and alert than his companion he sees danger much farther away, and gives notice of it, asking for the door to be shut by lightly pinching the mussel's gill. But this gratitude of the Crustacean towards a sympathetic bivalve is merely a hypothesis; we do not exactly know what passes in the intimacy of these two widely-differing natures.

For birds like the Cuckoo and the *Molothrus* it is not possible to plead attenuating circumstances. They occupy a place in an inhabited house without paying any sort of rent. Every one knows the Cuckoo's audacity. The female lays her eggs in different nests and troubles herself no further about their fate. She seeks for her offspring a shelter which she does not take the trouble to construct, and moreover at the same time assures for them the cares of a stranger in place of her own.

In North America a kind of Starling, the *Molothrus pecoris*, commonly called the Cow-bird, acts in the same careless fashion. It lives in the midst of herds, and owes its specific name to this custom; it feeds on the parasites on the skin of cattle. This bird constructs no nest. At the moment of laying the female seeks out an inhabited dwelling, and when the owner is absent she furtively lays an egg there. The young intruder breaks his shell after four days' incubation, that is to say, usually much before the legitimate children; and the parents, in order to silence the beak of the stranger who, without shame, claims his share with loud cries, neglect their own brood which have not yet appeared, and which they abandon. Their foster children repay them, however, with the blackest ingratitude. As soon as the little *Molothrus* feels his body covered with feathers and his little wings strong enough to sustain him he quits his adopted parents without consideration. These birds show a love of independence very rare among animals, with whom conjugal fidelity has become proverbial; they do not unite in couples; unions are free, and the mother hastens to deliver herself from the cares of bringing up her young in the manner we have seen. Two other species of *Molothrus* have the same habit, as have the American Cuckoo and the Golden Cuckoo of South Africa.

The habits of the *Molothrus bovariensis*, a closely allied Argentine Cow-bird, have been carefully studied by Mr. W. H. Hudson, who has also some interesting remarks as to the vestiges of the nesting instinct in this interesting parasitical bird, which now is constantly dropping eggs in all sorts of places, even on the ground, most of them being lost. "Before and during the breeding-season the females, sometimes accompanied by the males, are seen continually haunting and examining the domed nests of the *Dendrocolaptidæ.* This does not seem like a mere freak of curiosity, but their persistence in their investigations is precisely like that of birds that habitually make choice of such breeding-places. It is surprising that they never do actually lay in such nests, except when the side or dome has been accidentally broken enough to admit the light into the interior. Whenever I set boxes up in my trees, the female Cow-birds were the first to visit them. Sometimes one will spend half a day loitering about and inspecting a box, repeatedly climbing round and over it, and always ending at the entrance, into which she peers curiously, and when about to enter starting back, as if scared at the obscurity within. But after retiring a little space she will return again and again, as if fascinated by the comfort and security of such an abode. It is amusing to see how pertinaciously they hang about the ovens of the Oven-birds, apparently determined to take possession of them, flying back after a hundred repulses, and yet not entering them even when they have the opportunity. Sometimes one is seen following a Wren or a Swallow to its nest beneath the eaves, and then clinging to the wall beneath the hole into which it disappeared. That it is a recurrence to a long-disused habit I can scarcely doubt. I may mention that twice I have seen birds of this species attempting to build nests, and that on both occasions they failed to complete the work. So universal is the nest-making instinct that one might safely say the *M. bovariensis* had once possessed it, and that in the cases I have mentioned it was a recurrence, too weak to be efficient, to the ancestral habit." Mr. Hudson suggests that this bird lost the nest-making instinct by acquiring the semi-parasitical habit, common to many South American birds, of breeding in the large covered nests of the *Dendrocolaptidæ*, although, owing to increased severity in the struggle for the possession of such nests, this habit was defeated.[1]

The *Rhodius anarus*, a fish of European rivers, also ensures a quiet retreat for his offspring by a method which is not less indiscreet. At the period of spawning, a male chooses a female companion and with great vigilance keeps off all those who wish to approach her. When the laying becomes imminent, the *Rhodius*, swimming up and down at the bottom of the stream, at length discovers a *Unio*. The bivalve is asleep with his shell ajar, not suspecting the plot which is being formed against him. It is a question of nothing less than of transforming him into furnished lodgings. The female fish bears underneath her tail a prolongation of the oviduct; she introduces it delicately between the Mollusc's valves and allows an egg to fall between his branchial folds. In his turn the male approaches, shakes himself over it, and fertilises it. Then the couple depart in search of another *Unio*, to whom to confide another representative of the race. The egg, well sheltered against

[1] P. L. Sclater and W. H. Hudson, *Argentine Ornithology*, 1888, vol. i. pp. 72-86. A brief summary of the facts regarding parasitism among birds will be found in Girod's *Les Sociétés chez les Animaux*, 1891, pp. 287-294.

dangers from without, undergoes development, and one fine day the little fish emerges and frisks away from his peaceful retreat.

Other animals, more respectful of property, avoid using another's dwelling until it is abandoned by its proprietor, and no reproach of indelicacy can be addressed to the *Gobius minutus*, a fish which lives on our coasts at the mouth of rivers. The female lays beneath overturned shells, remains of Oysters, or Cardium shells. The valve is buried beneath several centimetres of sand, which supports it like a vault. It forms a solid roof, beneath which the eggs undergo their evolution. Sometimes the male remains by the little chamber to watch over their fate. It is possible to distinguish the two holes of entrance and exit which mark his habitual passage.

The Hermit-crab perhaps knows best how to take advantage of old clothes. (Fig. 19.) He collects shells of Gasteropods, abandoned flotsam, the first inhabitant of which has died. The Hermit-crab (*Pagurus Bernhardus*) is a Decapod Crustacean—that is to say, he resembles a very small Crab. But his inveterate habit during so many generations of sheltering his abdomen in a shell prevents this part from being encrusted with lime and becoming hard. The legs and the head remain in the ordinary condition outside the house, and the animal moves bearing it everywhere with him; on the least warning he retires into it entirely. But the Crustacean grows. When young he had chosen a small shell. A Mollusc, in growing, makes his house grow with him. The Hermit-crab cannot do this, and when his dwelling has become too narrow he abandons it for one that is more comfortable.

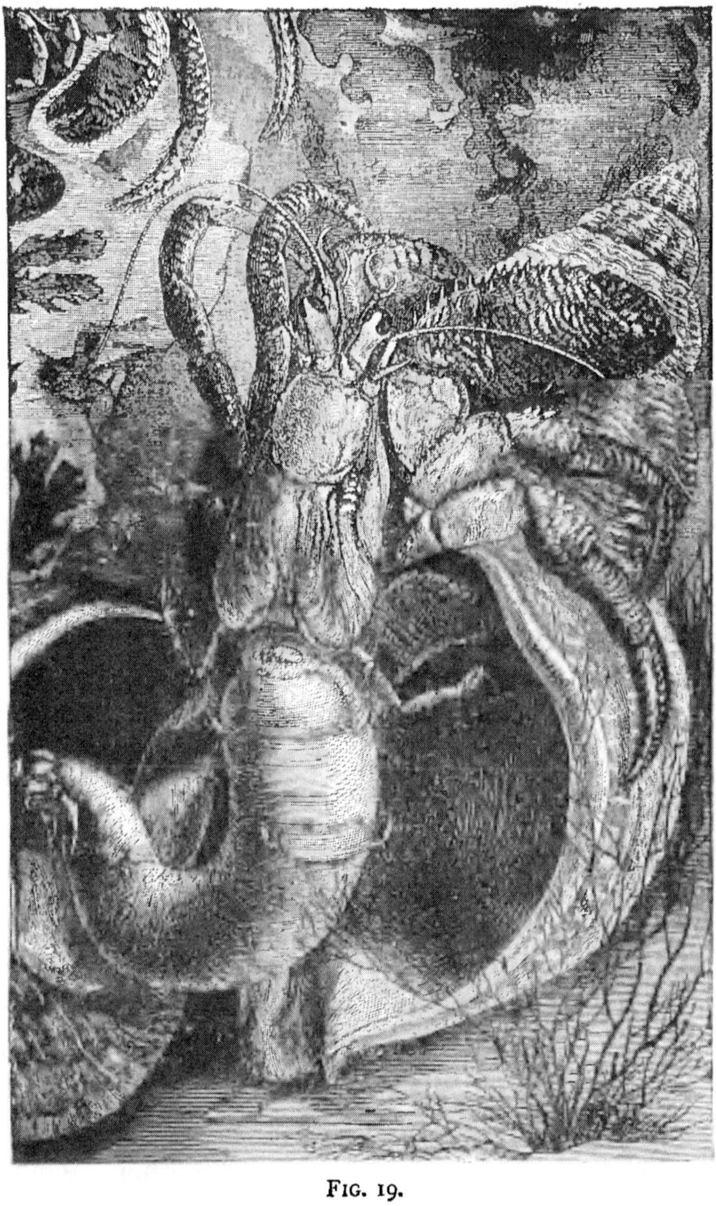

FIG. 19.

At first enclosed in the remains of a *Trochus*, he changes into that of a *Purpura;* a little later he seeks asylum in a Whelk. Beside the shelter which these shells assure to the Crustacean, they serve to mask his ferocity, and the prey which approaches confidently what it takes to be an inoffensive Mollusc, becomes his victim.

The Great Horned Owl likewise does not construct a nest; but takes possession of the dwellings abandoned by others. These birds utilise for laying their eggs sometimes the nest of a Crow or a Dove, sometimes the lair which a Squirrel had considered too dilapidated. The female, without troubling about the bad state of these ruins, or taking pains to repair them, lays her eggs here and sits on them.

*Classification of artificial shelters.*—It is time to turn to animals who have more regard for comfort, and who erect dwellings for themselves or their offspring. These dwellings may be divided into three groups: (1) Those which are hollowed in earth or in wood; (2) those which in the simplest form result from the division of material of any kind; then, as a complication, of materials bound together; then, as a last refinement, of delicate materials, such as blades of grass or threads of wool woven together; such are the nests of certain birds and the tents of nomads; (3) those which are built of moist earth which becomes hard on drying; the perfection of this method consists of piling up hard fragments, pieces of wood or ashlar, the moist earth being only a mortar which unites the hard parts together. Animals exercise with varying success these different methods, all of which Man still practises.

*Hollowed dwellings—Rudimentary burrows.*—We will first occupy ourselves with the dwelling hollowed in the earth. It is the least complicated form. The number of creatures who purely and simply bury themselves thus to obtain shelter is incalculable; I will only mention a few examples, and pass on from simple combinations to the more perfected industries, of which they present the first sketch.

It is known that at a certain epoch of the year Crabs abandon their hard carapaces. This phenomenon is known by the name of the moult; they remain in this condition for some time; it is the period during which they grow; then their integuments are encrusted anew with lime and again become resistant. While they are thus deprived of their ordinary protection they are exposed to a crowd of dangers, and they are so well aware of this that they remain hidden beneath rocks and pebbles. A crab of Guadeloupe, called *Gecarinus ruricola*, escapes the perils of this situation, thanks to its kind of life and its habit of hollowing out a burrow to live in while it is deprived of its habitual defence. This Crustacean lives on the earth, at a distance of about ten or twelve kilometres from the sea-shore, and nourishes itself on animal and vegetable remains. It approaches the water only at the period of laying eggs, turning towards the coast in the months of February and March. This migration does not take place, like some others, in compact bands; each follows the road in independence, and preserves a certain amount of liberty with regard to the path and the epoch of the journey. They lead an aquatic life till May or June; then the female abandons her little ones, who had begun their development attached to her claws, and they return to land. The moult takes place in August. At the approach of this dreaded crisis each hollows a hole between two roots, supplies it with green leaves, and carefully stops up the entrance. These labours accomplished, the crab is entirely sheltered; it undergoes the moult in safety, and does not emerge from its retreat until it is again capable of facing enemies, and of seizing food with its claws, which have become hard again. This seclusion appears to last a month. Here is, then, an example of a temporary dwelling rendered necessary by special conditions of defect for external life. We are here still in the infancy of the art.

Speaking generally, birds are accomplished architects. Certain of them are, however, content with a rudimentary cavern. There is no question here of those who retire to clefts in the rock or in trunks of trees, for in these cases the cavity is only the support of the true house, and it is in the construction of this that the artist reveals his talent. I wish to speak of animals which remain in a burrow without making a nest there. A Parroquet of New Zealand called the *Kakapo* (*Strigops habroptilus*) thus dwells in natural or hollowed excavations. It is only found in a restricted portion of the island and leads a miserable life there, habitually staying in the earth and pursued by numerous enemies, especially half-wild dogs. It tries to hold its own, but its wings and beak do not suffice to protect it, and the race would have completely disappeared if these birds were not able to resist, owing to the prudence with which they stay within their dwellings. They profit by a natural retreat, or one constructed in rocks or beneath roots of trees; they only come out when impelled by hunger, and return as soon as they can in case of danger.

A large number of animals also hollow out shelters for their eggs, with the double object of maintaining them at a constant temperature and of concealing them. Most reptiles act in this manner. The way in which a Tortoise, the *Cistudo lunaria*, prepares its nest is extremely curious. When the time for this labour arrives, the tortoise chooses a site. It commences by boring in the earth with the end of its tail, the muscles of which are held firmly contracted; it turns the tail like a gimlet and succeeds in making a conical hole. Gradually the depth of the hole becomes equal to the length of the tail, and the tool then becomes useless. The *Cistudo* enlarges the cavity with the help of its posterior legs. Using them alternately it withdraws the earth and kicks it away, then piles up this rubbish on the edge of the hole, arranging it so as to form a circular rampart. Soon the posterior members can take nothing more from the too distant bottom. The moment for laying has now come. As soon as the egg arrives at the cloaca one of the feet seizes it and lowers it gently into the nest, while the second foot seizes another egg, which during this time had appeared at the orifice. This manipulation lasts until the end of the operation, when the tortoise buries all its family, and to flatten the prominence which results she strikes it repeatedly with her plastron, raising herself on her legs.

It is not only land animals which adopt this custom of living in the earth, and there sheltering their offspring. Fish also make retreats on the bank or at the bottom. To mention only one case, the Bullhead

(*Cottus gobio*) of our rivers, which spawns in the Seine in May, June, and July, acts in this manner. Beneath a rock in the sand it prepares a cavity; then seeks females and brings them to lay eggs in its little lodging. During the four or five weeks before they come out it watches the eggs, keeping away as far as possible every danger which threatens them. It only leaves its position when pressed by hunger, and as soon as the hunt is concluded, returns to the post of duty.

Other animals when digging have a double object; they wish to shelter themselves, and at the same time to find the water which they need for themselves or for the development of their young.

It is well known that Frogs and Toads generally go in the spring to lay their eggs in streams and ponds. A Batrachian of Brazil and the hot regions of South America, the *Cystignathus ocellatus*, no doubt fearing too many dangers for the spawn if deposited in the open water, employs the artifice of hollowing, not far from the bank, a hole the bottom of which is filled by infiltration. It there places its eggs, and the little ones on their birth can lead an aquatic life while being guaranteed against its risks.

A terrestrial Crab, the *Cardisoma carnifex*, found in Bengal and the Antilles, acts in the same manner; but in this case it has in view its own convenience and not care for its offspring. Its habitat is especially in low-lying spots near the shore, where water may be found at a trifling depth beneath the soil. To establish its dwelling, the Crustacean first buries itself until it reaches the liquid level. Arrived at this point, it makes a large lair in the soft soil, and effects communication with the outside by various openings. It can thus easily come and go and retire into its cave, where it finds security and a humidity favourable for branchial respiration. From time to time it cleans out the dirt and rubbish which accumulate in the hole. It makes a little pile of all the refuse which it finds, and, seizing it between its claws and abdomen, carries it outside. Executing several journeys very rapidly, it soon clears out its dwelling.

The dipnoid *Protopterus*, which inhabits the marshes of Senegal and Gambia, is curious in more than one respect. Firstly, it can breathe oxygen, whether, like other fish, it finds it dissolved in water or in the atmospheric air. When during the summer the marshes in which it lives dry up, it takes refuge in the mud at the bottom, which hardens and imprisons it, and it thus remains curled up until the time when the water after the rainy season has softened the earth which surrounds it. This fact had been known for some time; travellers had brought back lumps of dried earth of varied size, the largest about as big as two fists. On opening them the same fish was always found within, and the chamber in which it is contained was lined with a sort of cocoon, having the appearance of dry gelatine. Duméril was able to observe one of these animals in captivity. At the period corresponding to the dry period of its own country, the *Protopterus* buried itself in the mud which had been placed at the bottom of the aquarium. In order to realise the conditions found in nature, the water which covered it was gradually withdrawn. The earth hardened in drying, and when broken the recluse was seen surrounded by hardened mucus, exactly like those which came from Senegal.

*Carefully-disposed burrows.*—All the cases which we have considered show us the industry of the hollowed dwelling in its primitive state; but other animals know how to furnish it with greater luxury. I will continue in the same order of increasing complication. Many beings live permanently in a burrow; Reptiles—Snakes or Lizards—are to be placed among these. Among others, the *Lacerta stirpium* arranges a narrow and deep hole, well hidden beneath a thicket, and retires into it for the winter, when cold renders it incapable of movement and at the mercy of its enemies. Before giving itself up to its hybernal sleep, it is careful to close hermetically the opening of the dwelling with a little earth and dried leaves. When spring returns and the heat awakens the reptile, it comes out to warm itself and to hunt, but never abandons its dwelling, always retiring into it in case of alarm and to pass there cold days and nights.

Darwin has observed and described[1] how a little Lacertilian, the *Conolophus subcristatus*, conducts its work of mining and digging. It establishes its burrow in a soft tufa, and directs it almost horizontally, hollowing it out in such a way that the axis of the hole makes a very small angle with the soil. This reptile does not foolishly expend its strength in this troublesome labour. It only works with one side of its body at a time, allowing the other side to rest. For instance, the right anterior leg sets to work digging, while the posterior leg on the same side throws out the earth. When fatigued, the left legs come into play, allowing the others to repose.

Other animals, without building their cavern with remarkable skill, show much sagacity in the choice of

[1] *Voyage of the Beagle.*

a site calculated to obtain certain determined advantages. In Egypt there are dogs which have become wild. Having shaken off the yoke of man, which in the East affords them little or no support, they lead an independent life. During the day they remain quiescent in desert spots or ruins, and at night they prowl about like jackals, hunting living prey or feeding on abandoned carcasses. There are hills which have in a manner become the property of these animals. They have founded villages there, and allow no one to approach. These hills have an orientation from north to south, so that one slope is exposed to the sun from morning to mid-day and the other from mid-day to evening. Now, dogs have a great horror of heat. They fear the torrid heat of the south as much as in our climate they like to lie warmed by gentle rays; there is no shadow too deep for their siesta. Therefore, on these Egyptian hills every dog hollows out a lair on both slopes. One of these dwellings is thus turned towards the east, the other towards the west. In the morning, when he returns from his nocturnal expeditions, the animal takes refuge in the second, and remains there until mid-day, sunk in refreshing sleep. At that hour the sun begins to reach him, and to escape it he passes over to the opposite slope; it is a curious sight to see them all, with pendent heads and sleepy air, advance with trailing steps to their eastern retreat, settle down in it, and continue their dream and their digestion till evening, when they again set forth to prowl. We never grow tired of admiring the intelligence of their domesticated fellows, but this trait seems to me worthy of remark; it proves a very developed power of observation and reflection.

The Trap-door Spiders of the south of Europe construct burrows which have been studied with great care and in much detail by Moggridge.[1] He found

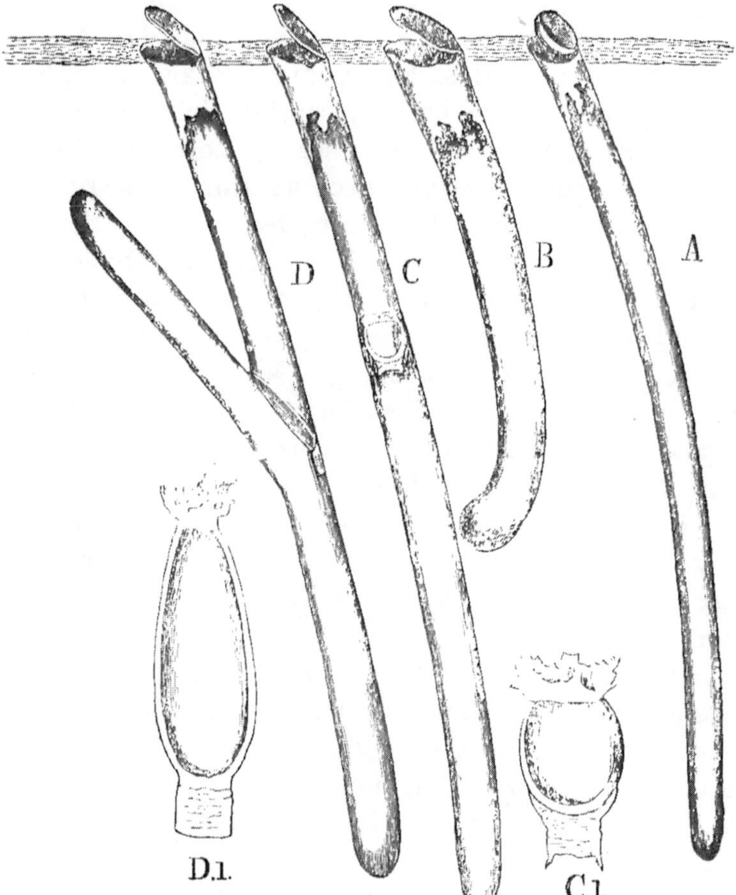


FIG. 20.

that there were four chief types of burrow, shown in the accompanying illustration (Fig 20) at about one-

[1] J. T. Moggridge, *Harvesting Ants and Trap-door Spiders*, contained in two elaborately illustrated volumes, London, 1873-74.

third the actual size (except C1 and D1, which are of natural size). While A and B have only one door, C and D, besides the surface door, have another a short way under ground. The whole burrow as well as the door are lined with silk, which also forms the hinge. The great art of the Trap-door Spider lies in her skilful forming of the door, which fits tightly, although it opens widely when she emerges, and which she frequently holds down when an intruder strives to enter, and in the manner with which the presence of the door is concealed, so as to harmonise with surrounding objects. Perhaps in no case is the concealment more complete than when dead leaves are employed to cover the door. In some cases a single withered olive leaf is selected, and it serves to cover the entrance; in other cases several are woven together with bits of wood or roots, as in the accompanying illustration, which represents such a door when open and when shut. (Fig. 21.)

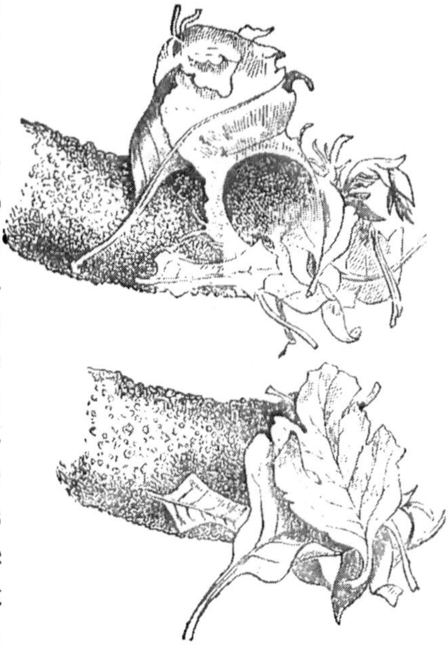

FIG. 21.

The Trap-door Spider (*Mygale henzii*, Girard), which is widely diffused in California, forms a simple shaft-like burrow, but, like the European Trap-door Spider, it is very skilful in forming an entrance and in concealing its presence. Its habits have lately been described by D. Cleveland of San Diego.[1] In the adobe land hillocks are numerous; they are about a foot in height, and some three or four feet in diameter. These hillocks are selected by the spiders —apparently because they afford excellent drainage, and cannot be washed away by the winter rains—and their stony summits are often full of spiders' nests. These subterranean dwellings are shafts sunk vertically in the earth, except where some stony obstruction compels the miner to deflect from a downward course. The shafts are from five to twelve inches in depth, and from one-half to one and a half inches in diameter, depending largely upon the age and size of the spider.

When the spider has decided upon a location, which is always in clay, adobe or stiff soil, he excavates the shaft by means of the sharp horns at the end of his mandibles, which are his pick and shovel and mining tools. The earth is held between the mandibles and carried to the surface. When the shaft is of the required size, the spider smoothes and glazes the wall with a fluid which is secreted by itself. Then the whole shaft is covered with a silken paper lining, spun from the animal's spinnarets.

The door at the top of the shaft is made of several alternate layers of silk and earth, and is supplied with an elastic and ingenious hinge, and fits closely in a groove around the rim of the tube. This door simulates the surface on which it lies, and is distinguishable from it only by a careful scrutiny. The clever spider even glues earth and bits of small plants

[1] *Science*, 20th January 1893.

on the upper side of his trap-door, thus making it closely resemble the surrounding surface.

The spider generally stations itself at the bottom of the tube. When, by tapping on the door, or by other means, a gentle vibration is caused, the spider runs to the top of his nest, raises the lid, looks out and reconnoitres. If a small creature is seen, it is seized and devoured. If the invader is more formidable, the door is quickly closed, seized and held down by the spider, so that much force is required to lever it open. Then, with the intruder looking down upon him, the spider drops to the bottom of his shaft.

It has been found by many experiments that when the door of his nest is removed, the spider can renew it five times—never more than that. Within these limitations, the door torn off in the evening was found replaced by a new one in the morning. Each successive renewal showed, however, a greater proportion of earth, and a smaller proportion of silk, until finally the fifth door had barely enough silk to hold the earth together. The sixth attempt, if made, was a failure, because the spinnarets had exhausted their supply of the web fluid. When the poor persecuted spider finds his domicile thus open and defenceless, he is compelled to leave it, and wait until his stock of web fluid is renewed.[1]

Skilful diggers prepare burrows with several entrances; some even arrange several rooms, each for a special object. The Otter seeks its food in the water,

[1] The Trap-door Spiders of various parts of the world have been carefully studied, and the gradual development of their skill traced through various species, by Eugène Simon ; see, for example, *Actes de la Soc. Lin. de Bordeaux*, 1888.

and actively hunts fish in ponds and rivers. But when fishing is over, it likes to keep dry and at the same time sheltered from terrestrial enemies. Its dwelling must also present an easy opening into the water. In order to fulfil all these conditions, its house consists first of a large room hollowed in the bank at a level sufficiently high to be beyond reach of floods. From the bottom of this keep a passage starts which sinks and opens about fifty centimetres beneath the surface of the water. It is through here that the Otter noiselessly glides to find himself in the midst of his hunting domain without having been seen or been obliged to make a noisy plunge which would put the game to flight. If this were all, the hermetically-closed dwelling would soon become uninhabitable, as there would be no provision for renewing the air, so the Otter proceeds to form a second passage from the ceiling of the room to the ground, thus forming a ventilation tube. In order that this may not prove a cause of danger, it is always made to open up in the midst of brushwood or in a tuft of rushes and reeds.

Marmots also are not afraid of the work which will assure them a warm and safe refuge in the regions they inhabit, where the climate is rough. In summer they ascend the Alps to a height of 2,500 to 3,000 metres and rapidly hollow a burrow like that for winter time, which I am about to describe, but smaller and less comfortable. They retire into it during bad weather or to pass the night. When the snow chases them away and causes them to descend to a lower zone, they think about constructing a genuine house in which to shut themselves during the winter and to sleep. Twelve or fifteen of these little animals unite their efforts to make first a horizontal passage, which may reach the length of three or four metres. They enlarge the extremity of it into a vaulted and circular room more than two metres in diameter. They make there a good pile of very dry hay on which they all install themselves, after having carefully protected themselves against the external cold by closing up the passage with stones and calking the interstices with grass and moss.

In solitary woods or roads the Badger (*Meles*), who does not like noise, prepares for himself a peaceful retreat, clean and well ventilated, composed of a vast chamber situated about a metre and a half beneath the surface. He spares no pains over it, and makes it communicate with the external world by seven or eight very long passages, so that the points where they open are about thirty paces distant from one another. In this way, if an enemy discovers one of them and introduces himself into the Badger's home, the Badger can still take flight through one of the other passages. In ordinary times they serve for the aëration of the central room. The animal attaches considerable importance to this. He is also very clean in his habits, and every day may be seen coming out for little walks, having an object of an opposite nature to the search for food. This praiseworthy habit is, as we shall see, exploited by the Fox in an unworthy manner.

The Fox has many misdeeds on his conscience, but his conduct towards the Badger is peculiarly indelicate. The Fox is a skilful digger, and when he cannot avoid it, he can hollow out a house with several rooms. The dwelling has numerous openings, both as a measure of prudence and of hygiene, for this arrangement enables the air to be renewed. He prepares several chambers side by side; one of which he uses for observation and to take his siesta in; a second as a sort of larder in which he piles up what he cannot devour at once; a third, in which the female brings forth and rears her young. But he does not hesitate to avoid this labour when possible. If he finds a rabbit warren he tries first to eat the inhabitants, and then, his mind cleared from this anxiety, arranges their domicile to his own taste, and comfortably installs himself in it. In South America, again, the Argentine Fox frequently takes up permanent residence in a vizcachera, ejecting the rightful owners; he is so quiet and unassuming in his manners that the vizcachas become indifferent to his presence, but in spring the female fox will seize on the young vizcachas to feed her own young, and if she has eight or nine, the young of the whole village of vizcachas may be exterminated.

The Badger's dwelling appears to the Fox particularly enviable. In order to dislodge the proprietor he adopts the following plan. Knowing that the latter can tolerate no ordure near his home, he chooses as a place of retirement one of the passages which lead to the chamber of the peaceful recluse. He insists repeatedly, until at last the Badger, insulted by this grossness, and suffocated by the odour, decides to move elsewhere and hollow a fresh palace. The Fox is only waiting for this, and installs himself without ceremony.

The Vizcacha (*Lagostomus trichodactylus*) is a large Rodent inhabiting a vast extent of country in the pampas of La Plata, Patagonia, etc. Unlike most other burrowing species, the Vizcacha prefers to work on open level spots. On the great grassy plains it is even able to make its own conditions, like the Beaver, and is in this respect, and in its highly-developed social instinct, among the two or three Mammals which approach Man, although only a Rodent, and even in this order, according to Waterhouse, coming very low down by reason of its marsupial affinities.

The Vizcacha lives in small communities of from twenty to thirty members, in a village of deep-chambered burrows, some twelve or fifteen in number, with large pit-like entrances closely grouped together, and as the Vizcachera, as this village is called, endures for an indefinitely long period, the earth which is constantly brought up forms an irregular mound thirty or forty feet in diameter, and from fifteen to thirty inches above the level of the road; this mound serves to protect the dwelling from floods on low ground. A clearing is made all round the abode and all rubbish thrown on the mound; the Vizcachas thus have a smooth turf on which to disport themselves, and are freed from the danger of lurking enemies.

The entire village occupies an area of one hundred to two hundred square feet of ground. The burrows vary greatly in extent; usually in a Vizcachera there are several that, at a distance of from four to six feet from the entrance, open into large circular chambers. From these chambers other burrows diverge in all directions, some running horizontally, others obliquely downwards to a maximum depth of six feet from the surface; some of these galleries communicate with those of other burrows.

On viewing a Vizcachera closely, the first thing that strikes the observer is the enormous size of the entrances to the central burrows in the mound; there are usually several smaller outside burrows. The entrance to some of the principal burrows is sometimes four to six feet across the mouth, and sometimes it is deep enough for a tall man to stand in up to the waist.

It is not easy to tell what induces a Vizcacha to found a new community, for they increase very slowly, and are very fond of each other's society. It is invariably one individual alone who founds the new village. If it were for the sake of better pasture he would remove to a considerable distance, but he merely goes from forty to sixty yards off to begin operations. Sooner or later, perhaps after many months, other individuals join the solitary Vizcacha, and they become the parents of innumerable generations in the same village: old men, who have lived all their lives in one district, remember that many of the Vizcacheras around them existed when they were children.

It is always a male who begins the new village. Although he does not always adopt the same method, he usually works very straight into the earth, digging a hole twelve or fourteen inches wide, but not so deep, at an angle of about 25° with the surface. After he has progressed inwards for a few feet, the animal is no longer content merely to scatter the loose earth; he cleans it away in a straight line from the entrance, and scratches so much on this line, apparently to make the slope gentler, that he soon forms a trench a foot or more in depth, and often three or four feet in length. This facilitates the conveyance of the loose earth as far as possible from the entrance of the burrow. But after a while the animal is unwilling that earth should accumulate even at the end of this long passage, and proceeds to form two additional trenches, making an acute or right angle converging into the first trench, so that the whole when completed takes a Y shape. These trenches are continually deepened and lengthened in this manner, the angular segment of earth between them being scratched away, until by degrees it gives place to one large deep irregular mouth. The burrows are made best in the black and red moulds of the pampas; but even in such soils the entrances may be varied. In some the central trench is wanting, or so short that there appear to be but two passages converging directly into the burrow, or these two trenches may be so curved inwards as to form the segment of a circle. Usually, however, the varieties are only modifications of the Y-shaped system.

On the pampas a wide-mouthed burrow possesses a distinct advantage over the more usual shape. The two outer trenches diverge so widely from the mouth that half the earth brought out is cast behind instead of before it, thus creating a mound of equal height about the entrance, by which it is secured from water during great rainfalls, while cattle avoid treading over the great pit-like entrances, though they soon tread and break in the burrows of the Armadillo and other species when these make their homes on perfectly level ground.

The Vizcachas do not usually leave their burrows until dark, but in summer they come out before sunset. Usually one of the old males first appears, and sits on some prominent place on the mound, apparently in no haste to begin his evening meal. Other Vizcachas soon begin to appear, each quietly taking up his position at the burrow's mouth. The females, known by their smaller size and lighter colour, sit upright on their haunches, as if to command a better view; they are always wilder and sprightlier in their gestures than the males. They view a human stranger with a mixture of fear and curiosity, sometimes allowing him to come within five or six paces of them; in desert regions, however, where enemies are numerous, the Vizcacha is very timid and wary.

These animals are very sociable, and their sociability extends beyond their own vizcachera. On approaching a vizcachera at night, usually some of the Vizcachas on it scamper off to distant burrows. These are neighbours merely come to pay a friendly visit. The intercourse is so frequent that little straight paths are formed from one village to another. Their social instinct leads members of one village to assist those of another when in trouble. Thus, if a vizcachera is covered over with earth in order to destroy the animals within, Vizcachas from distant burrows will subsequently be found zealously digging out their friends. The hospitality of the Vizcacha does not, however, extend to his burrow; he has a very strong feeling with regard to the sanctity of the burrow. A Vizcacha never enters another's burrow, and if by chance driven into one by dogs will emerge speedily, apparently finding that the danger within is greater than the danger without. In connection with the sociability of the Vizcacha, we must take into consideration the fact that Vizcachas possess a wonderfully varied and expressive language, and are engaged in perpetual discussion all night long.[1]

[1] The Vizcacha has been carefully studied by Mr. W. H. Hudson, whose account has here been closely followed, *Proceedings of the Zoological Society*, 1872, and *Naturalist in La Plata*, 1892, pp. 289-313.

*Burrows with barns adjoined.*—Certain Rodents have carried hollow dwellings to great perfection. Among these the Hamster of Germany (*Cricetus frumentarius*) is not the least ingenious. To his dwelling-room he adds three or four storehouses for the amassed provisions of which I have already had occasion to speak. The burrow possesses two openings: one, which the animal prefers to use, which sinks vertically into the soil; the other, the passage of exit with a gentle and very winding slope. The bottom of the central room is carpeted with moss and straw, which make it a warm and pleasant home. A third tunnel starts from this sleeping chamber, soon forking and leading to the wheat barns. Thus during the winter the Hamster has no pressing need to go out except on fine days for a little fresh air. He has everything within his reach, and can remain shut up with nothing to fear from the severity of the season.

*Dwellings hollowed out in wood.*—It is not only the soil which may serve for retreat; wood serves as an asylum for numerous animals, who bore it, and find in it both food and shelter. In this class must be placed a large number of Worms, Insects, and Crustaceans. One of these last, the *Chelura terebrans*, a little Amphipod, constitutes a great danger for the works of man. It attacks piles sunken to support structures, and undermines them to such a degree that they eventually fall. Wood is formed of concentric layers alternately composed of large vessels formed during the summer, and smaller vessels formed during the winter. The latter zones are more resistant, the former are softer. When one of these Crustaceans attacks a pile, it first bores a little horizontal passage, stopping at a layer of summer-growth. It there hollows a large grotto, leaving here and there pillars of support. It lays in this space. The new generation working around the parents increases the space and feeds on the wood removed. A second generation is produced, and the inhabitants become pressed for space. The new-born pierce numerous passages and penetrate towards the interior of the pile as far as the next summer layer. There they spread themselves, always boring; they construct new rooms like the first, and arrange pillars here and there. Their descendants gain the subjacent zone, and so the process goes on. During this time the early ancestors who hollowed the surface dwellings have died, and the holes which they made are no longer habitable; but they have all contributed to diminish the resistance of the wood, and this continues as long as the race which they produced makes its way towards the centre of the stake.

An insect, the *Xylocopa violacea* (Fig. 22), related to our Humble-bee, from which it differs in several anatomical characters, and by the dark violet tint of its wings, brings an improvement to the formation of the shelter which it makes in wood for its larvæ. Instead of hollowing a mere retreat to place there all its eggs indiscriminately, it divides them into compartments, separated by horizontal partitions. It is the female alone who accomplishes this task, connected with the function of perpetuating the race. She chooses an old tree-trunk, a pole, or the post of a fence, exposed to the sun and already worm-eaten, so that her labour may be lightened. She first attacks the wood perpendicularly to the surface, then suddenly turns and directs downwards the passage, the diameter of which is about equal to the size of the insect's body. The *Xylocopa* thus forms a tube about thirty centimetres in length. Quite at the bottom she places the first egg, leaving beside it a provision of honey necessary to nourish the larva during its evolution ; she then closes it with a partition. This partition is made with fragments of the powder of wood glued together with saliva. A first horizontal

FIG. 22.

ring is applied round the circumference of the tube ; then in the interior of this first ring a second is formed, and so on continuously, until the central opening, more and more reduced, is at last entirely closed up. This ceiling forms the floor for the next chamber, in which the female deposits a new egg, provided, like the other, with abundant provisions. The same acts are repeated until the retreat becomes transformed into a series of isolated cells in which the larvæ can effect their development, and from which they will emerge either by themselves perforating a thin wall which separates them from daylight, or by an opening which the careful mother has left to allow them to attain liberty without trouble.[1]

*Woven dwellings.*—The second class of habitation, which I have called the woven dwelling, proceeds at first from the parcelling up of substances, then of objects capable of being entangled like wisps of wood or straw, then of fine and supple materials which the artisan can work together in a regular manner, that is to say by felting or weaving. Facts will show us the successive stages of improvement which have been introduced into this industry. I will begin with the more rudimentary.

*Rudiments of this industry.*—There are, first, cases in which the will of the animal does not intervene, or at least is very slightly manifested. The creature is found covered and protected by foreign bodies which are often living beings. Spider-crabs (*Maïa*), for example, have their carapaces covered with algæ and hydroids of all sorts. Thus garnished, the Crustaceans have the advantage of not being recognised from afar when they go hunting, since beneath this fleece they resemble some rock. H. Fol has observed at Villefranche-sur-Mer a *Maïa* so buried beneath this vegetation that it was impossible at first sight to distinguish it from the stones around. Under these conditions the animal submits to a shelter rather than creates it. Yet it is not so passive as one might at first be led to suppose. When the algæ which

[1] Réaumur, *Memoires pour servir à l'histoire des Insectes*, pp. 97 *et seq.*

flourish on its back become too long and impede or delay its progress, it tears them off with its claws and thoroughly cleans itself. The carapace being quite clean, the animal finds itself too smooth and too easy to distinguish from surrounding objects; it therefore takes up again fragments of algæ and replaces them where they do not delay to take root like cuttings and to flourish anew. This culture is therefore intentional; the crab directs it and arrests its exuberance; it is no more the victim of it than the gardener is the slave of the vegetables which he waters day by day. From generation to generation this crab has acquired the habit, the instinct if one prefers, of thus covering itself so that it may be confused with neighbouring objects. Naturally it is ignorant of botany, and knows nothing of cuttings. If placed in an aquarium with little fragments of paper it will seize them and place them on its back, as it would have done with algæ, without troubling as to whether they become fixed or not. In spite of this lack of judgment, we cannot fail to recognise in this *Maïa* a certain ingenuity in self-concealment.

The Sponge-crab (*Dromia vulgaris*) also practises this method of shelter. It seizes a large sponge and maintains it firmly over its carapace with the help of the posterior pair of limbs. The sponge continues to prosper and to spread over the Crustacean who has adopted it. (Fig. 23.) The two beings do not seem to be definitely fixed to each other; the contact of a sudden wave will separate them. When the divorce is effected, the *Dromia* immediately throws itself on its cherished covering and replaces it. M. Künckel d'Herculais tells of one of these curious crustaceans which delighted the workers in the laboratory of Concarneau. The need for covering them-

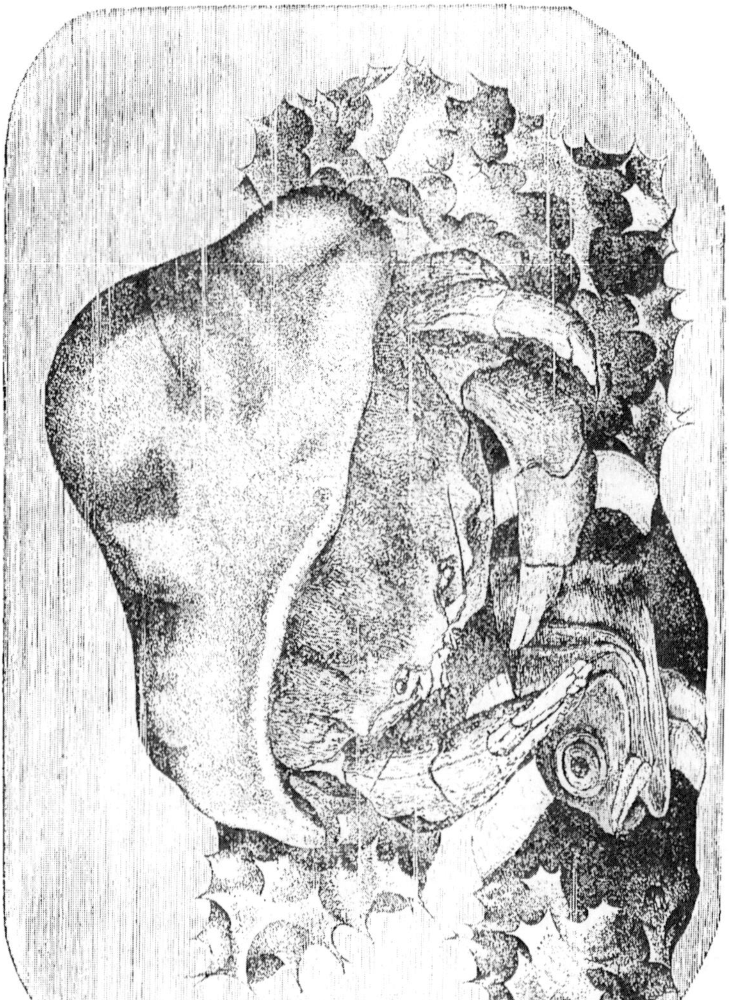

Fig. 23.

selves experienced by these Crabs is so strong that in aquariums when their sponge is taken away they will apply to the back a fragment of wrack or of anything which comes to hand. A little white cloak with the arms of Brittany was manufactured for one of these captives, and it was very amusing to see him put on his overcoat when he had nothing else wherewith to cover himself.[1]

In these two cases which I have brought forward to exhibit the rudiments of this industry, the animals' reflection and will play but a small part; even in the *Dromia* custom is so inveterate in the race that it has reacted on the animal's organisation, and its four posterior legs are profoundly modified for the purpose of firmly holding the sheltering sponge; they no longer serve for swimming or walking. The animals of which I have now to speak possess more initiative; although all do not act with the same success, or show themselves equally skilful. Let us turn first to the least experienced.

An Australian bird, the *Catheturus Lathami*, as described by Gould, is still in the rudiments, and limits itself to preparing an enormous pile of leaves. It begins its work some weeks before laying its eggs; with its claws it pushes behind it all the dead leaves which fall on the earth and brings them into a heap. The bird throws new material on the summit until the hole is of suitable height. This detritus ferments when left to itself, and a gentle heat is developed in the centre of the edifice. The *Catheturus* returns to lay near this coarse shelter; it then takes each egg and buries it in the heap, the larger end uppermost. It places a new layer above, and quits its labour for good. Incubation takes place favoured by the uniform heat of this decomposing

[1] Brehm, édition Française, *Crustacés*, p. 738.

mass, hatching is produced, and the young emerge from their primitive nest.

Birds are not alone in constructing temporary dwellings in which to lay their eggs ; some Fish are equally artistic in this kind of industry, and even certain Reptiles. The Alligator of the Mississippi would not perhaps at first be regarded as a model of maternal foresight. Yet the female constructs a genuine nest. She seeks a very inaccessible spot in the midst of brushwood and thickets of reeds. With her jaw she carries thither boughs which she arranges on the soil and covers with leaves. She lays her eggs and conceals them with care beneath vegetable remains. Not yet considering her work completed, she stays in the neighbourhood watching with jealous eye the thicket which shelters the dear deposit, and never ceases to mount guard threateningly until the day when her young ones can follow her into the stream.

FIG. 24.

A hymenopterous relative of the Bees, the *Megachile*, cuts out in rose-leaves fragments of appropriate form which it bears away to a small hole in a tree, an abandoned mouse nest or some similar cavity. There it rolls them, works them up, and arranges them with much art, so as to manufacture what resemble thimbles, which it fills with honey and in which it lays.[1] (Fig. 24.)

[1] Réaumur, *Memoires pour servir à l'histoire des Insectes*, pp. 97 *et seq.*

The *Anthocopa* acts in a similar manner, carpeting the holes of which it takes possession with the delicate petals of the corn poppy.

The retreats of nocturnal birds of prey do not differ in method of construction from these two kinds of nests. They are holes in trees, in ruins, in old walls, and are lined with soft and warm material. These dwellings are related, not to the type of the hollowed cave, but to that of the habitation manufactured from mingled materials. They constitute an inferior form in which the pieces are not firmly bound together but need support throughout. The cavity is the support which sustains the real house.

*Dwellings formed of coarsely-entangled materials.*— Diurnal birds of prey are the first animals who practise skilfully the twining of materials. Their nests, which have received the name of eyries, are not yet masterpieces of architecture, and reveal the beginning of the industry which is pushed so far by other birds. Usually situated in wild and inaccessible spots, the young are there in safety when their parents are away on distant expeditions. The abrupt summits of cliffs and the tops of the highest forest trees are the favourite spots chosen by the great birds of prey. The eyrie generally consists of a mass of dry branches which cross and mutually support one another, constituting a whole which is fairly resistant.

Even these primitive nests are not, however, without more complicated details of interest. Thus Mr. Denis Gale wrote to Bendire concerning the Golden Eagle in America: "Here in Colorada, in the numerous glades running from the valleys into the foothills, high inaccessible ledges are quite frequently met with which afford the Eagles secure sites for their enormous nests. I know of one nest that must contain two waggon-loads of material. It is over seven feet high, and quite six feet wide on its upper surface. In most cases the cliff above overhangs the site. At the end of February or the beginning of March, the needful repairs to the nest are attended to, and the universal branch of evergreen is laid upon the nest, seemingly for any purpose save that of utility. This feature has been present in all the nests I have examined myself, or have had examined by others; it would seem to be employed as a badge of occupancy."[1] This curious feature is also found in the nests of the Bald or American Eagle. Thus Dr. W. L. Ralph furnished Bendire with the following observations made in Florida on the dwellings of this, the national bird of the United States:—"The nests are immense structures, from five to six feet in diameter, and about the same in depth, and so strong that a man can walk around in one without danger of breaking through; in fact, my assistant would always get in the nest before letting the eggs down to me. They are composed of sticks, some of which are two or three inches thick, and are lined with marsh grass or some similar material. There is usually a slight depression in the centre, where the eggs are placed, but the edge of the nest extends so far beyond this that it is almost impossible to see the bird from below, unless it has its head well up. I have frequently found foreign substances in their nests, usually placed on the edges of it, the object of which I cannot account for. Often it would be a ball of grass, wet or dry, sometimes a green branch from a pine tree, and again a piece of wood, bark, or other

[1] *Life Histories of North American Birds*, 1892, p. 265.

material. It seemed as if they were placed in the nests as if to mark them. From its frequent occurrence, at least, it seemed to me as if designedly done."[1]

The abodes of Squirrels, though exhibiting more art, are constructions of the same nature; that is to say, they are formed of interlaced sticks. This animal builds its home to shelter itself there in the bad season, to pass the night in it, and to rear its young. Very agile, and not afraid of climbing, it places its domicile near the tops of our highest forest trees. Rather capricious also, and desiring change of residence from time to time, it builds several of them; at least three or four, sometimes more. The materials which it needs are collected on the earth among fallen dead branches, or are torn away from the old abandoned nest of a crow or some other bird. The Squirrel firsts builds a rather hollow floor by intermingling the fragments of wood which it has brought. In this state its dwelling resembles a magpie's nest. But the fastidious little animal wishes to be better protected and not thus to sleep in the open air. Over this foundation he raises a conical roof; the sticks which form it are very skilfully disposed, and so well interlaced that the whole is impenetrable to rain. The house must still be furnished, and this is done with oriental luxury; that is to say, the entire furniture consists of a carpet, a carpet of very dry moss, which the Squirrel tears from the trunks of trees, and which it piles up so as to have a soft and warm couch. An entrance situated at the lower part gives access to the aërial castle; it is usually directed towards the east. On the opposite side there is

[1] *Life Histories of American Birds*, p. 275.

another orifice by which the animal can escape if an enemy should invade the principal entrance. In ordinary times also it serves to ventilate the chamber by setting up a slight current of air. The Squirrel greatly fears storms and rain, and during bad weather hastens to take refuge in his dwelling. If the wind blows in the direction of the openings, the little beast at once closes them with two stoppers of moss, and keeps well shut in as long as the storm rages.

The great Anthropoid Apes have found nothing better for shelter than the Squirrels' method. It must, however, be taken into account that they have much more difficulty in arranging and maintaining much heavier rooms, and in building up a shelter with larger surface.

The Orang-outang, which lives in the virgin forests of the Sunda Archipelago, does not feel the need of constructing a roof against the rain. He is content with a floor established in the midst of a tree, and made of broken and interlaced branches. He piles up on this support a considerable mass of leaves and moss; for the Orang does not sleep seated like the other great apes, but lies down in the manner of Man, as has often been observed when he is in captivity. When he feels the cold he is ingenious enough to cover himself with the leaves of his couch.

In Upper and Lower Guinea the Chimpanzee (*Troglodytes niger*) also establishes his dwelling on trees. He first makes choice of a large horizontal branch, which constitutes a sufficient floor for the agile animal. Above this branch he bends the neighbouring boughs, crosses them, and interlaces them so as to obtain a sort of framework. When this preliminary labour is accomplished, he collects dead wood or breaks up branches and adds them to the first. Before commencing he had taken care when choosing the site that the whole was so arranged that a fork was within reach to sustain the roof. He thus constructs a very sufficient shelter. These apes are sociable and prefer to live in each other's neighbourhood. They even go on excursions in rather large bands. Notwithstanding this, more than one or two cabins are never seen on the same tree; perhaps this is because the complicated conditions required for the construction are not likely to be realised several times on the same tree; perhaps also it is a desire for independence which impels the Chimpanzees not to live too near to each other.[1]

The *Troglodytes calvus*, a relative of the preceding, inhabiting the same regions, as described by Du Chaillu, shows still more skill in raising his roof. A tree is always chosen for support. He breaks off boughs and fastens them by one end to the trunk, by the other to a large branch. To fix all these pieces he employs very strong creepers, which grow in abundance in his forests. Above this framework, which indicates remarkable ingenuity, the animal piles up large leaves, forming in layers well pressed down and quite impenetrable to the rain. The whole has the appearance of an open parasol. The ape sits on a branch beneath his handiwork, supporting himself against the trunk with one arm. He has thus an excellent shelter against the mid-day sun as well as against tropical showers. Male and female each

[1] Savage, "Observations on the External Characters and Habits of the *Troglodytes niger*," *Boston Journal Nat. Hist.*, 1843, pp. 362-376.

possess a dwelling on two neighbouring trees, the principle of conjugal cohabitation not being admitted in this species. As to the child, it appears that it sleeps near its mother, until it is of age to lead an independent life.

There exists in Australia, the country of zoological singularities, a bird with very curious customs. This is the Satin Bower-bird. The art displayed in this bird's constructions is not less interesting than the sociability he gives evidence of, and his desire to have for his hours of leisure a shelter adorned to his taste. The bowers which he constructs, and which present on a small scale the appearance of the arbours in our old gardens, are places for re-union and for warbling and courtship, in which the birds stay during the day, when no anxiety leads them to disperse. They are not, properly speaking, nests built for the purpose of rearing young; for at the epoch of love each couple separates and constructs a special retreat in the neighbourhood of the bower. These shelters are always situated in the most retired parts of the forest, and are placed on the earth at the foot of trees. Several couples work together to raise the edifice, the males performing the chief part of the work. At first they establish a slightly convex floor, made with interlaced sticks, intended to keep the place sheltered from the moisture of the soil. The arbour rises in the centre of this first platform. Boughs vertically arranged are interlaced at the base with those of the floor. The birds arrange them in two rows facing each other; they then curve together the upper extremities of these sticks, and fix them so as to obtain a vault. All the prominences in the materials employed are turned towards the outside, so that the interior of the room may be smooth and the birds may not catch their plumage in it. This done, the little architects, to embellish their retreat, transport to it a number of conspicuous objects, such as very white stones from a neighbouring stream, shells, the bright feathers of the parroquet, whatever comes to their beak. All these treasures are arranged on the earth, before the two entries to the bower, so as to form on each side a carpet, which is not smooth, but the varied colours of which rejoice the eye. The prettiest treasures are fixed into the wall of the hut. These houses of pleasure, with all their adornments, form a dwelling very much to the taste of this winged folk, and the birds pass there the greater part of the day, preening their feathers and narrating the news of the forest. Bower-birds' clubs are drawing-rooms raised at the common expense by all who frequent them. The Spotted Bower-bird, the *Chlamydera maculata*, which also lives in the interior of Australia, exercises this method of construction with equal success. The bowers built by these birds may be one metre in length; this is on a very luxurious scale, the animal itself only measuring twenty-five centimetres. In this species, as among other Bower-birds, the bowers are not the labour and the property of a single couple; they are the result of the collaboration of several households, who come together to shelter themselves there. These birds feed only on grains, so that it is to a very pronounced taste for collecting that we must attribute this mania of piling up before the entrance of the bower white stones, shells, and small bones. (Fig. 25.) These objects are intended solely for the delight of these feathered artists. They are very careful also only to collect pieces which have been whitened and dried by the sun.[1]

Certain Humming-birds also; according to Gould, decorate their dwellings with great taste. "They instinctively fasten thereon," he stated, "beautiful pieces of flat lichen, the larger pieces in the middle, and the smaller on the part attached to the branch. Now and then a pretty feather is intertwined or fastened to the outer sides, the stem being always so placed that the feather stands out beyond the surface."[2]

*Dwellings woven of flexible substances.*—In spite of their lack of skill and the inadequacy of their organs for this kind of work, Fish are not the most awkward architects. The species which construct nests for laying in are fairly numerous; the classical case of the Stickleback is always quoted, but this is not the only animal of its class to possess the secret of the manufacture of a shelter for its eggs.

A fish of Java, the Gourami (*Osphronemus olfax*), establishes an ovoid nest with the leaves of aquatic plants woven together. It makes its work about the size of a fist, takes no rest until it is completed, and is able to finish it in five or six days. It is the male alone who weaves this dwelling; when it is ready a female comes to lay there, and generally fills it; it may contain from six hundred to a thousand eggs.

In the sea of Sargasso lives a fish which has received the name of the *Antennarius marmoratus*. Its

[1] Gould first accurately described the habits of the Bower-birds, *Proceed. Zool. Soc., London*, 1840, p. 94; also *Handbook to the Birds of Australia* (1865), vol. i. pp. 444-461. See also Darwin's *Descent of Man* (1881), pp. 381 and 413-414.

[2] Gould, *Introduction to the Trochilidæ*, 1861, p. 19.

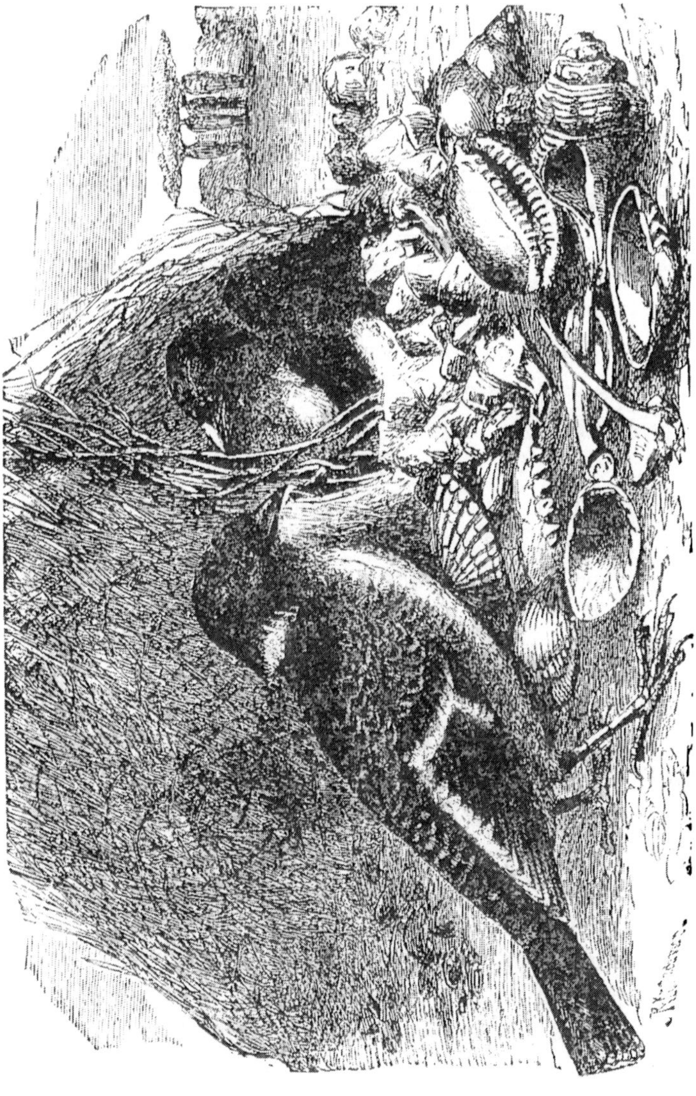

Fig. 25.

flattened and monstrous head gives it a strange aspect, and it is marbled with brown and yellow. These colours are those of the tufts of floating sea-weed around it, and, thanks to this arrangement, it can easily hide itself amid them without being recognised from afar. This animal constructs for its offspring a fairly safe retreat. The materials which it employs are tufts of Sargasso so abundant in this portion of the Atlantic. It collects all the filaments, and unites them solidly by surrounding them with viscous mucus which it secretes and which hardens. When its work is sufficiently firm not to be destroyed by the waves it lays its eggs in it, and the floating nest is abandoned to its fate. The little ones come out and find within it a sufficient protection for their early age. These dwellings thus floating on the surface of the sea are rounded and about the size of a cocoa-nut.

In Guiana and Brazil another species, the *Chœstostomus pictus*, is found, which is equally skilful. With aquatic plants it constructs a spherical nest and arranges it in the midst of the reeds, level with the water. At the lower part a hole is left, through which the female comes to lay. After fertilisation, the couple, as is rarely found among fish, remain in the neighbourhood of their offspring to assist them if necessary. This praiseworthy sentiment is often the cause of their ruin. The inhabitants of the banks speculate on the love of these fish for their offspring to gain possession of them. It is sufficient to place a basket near the entrance of the dwelling, which is then lightly struck. The animal, threatened in its affections, darts furiously forward with bristling spines and throws itself into the trap.

It is scarcely necessary to recall the skilful art with which the Stickleback which inhabits all our streams plaits its nest and remains sentinel near it. (Fig. 26.) This fish has indeed monopolised our admiration, and is considered as the most skilful, if not the only aquatic architect. Yet, besides those which I have already mentioned, there is one which equals the Stickleback in the skill it displays in constructing a shelter for its spawn. This is the *Gobius niger* met on our coasts, especially in the estuaries of rivers. The male interlaces and weaves the leaves of algæ, etc., and when he has finished his preparations, he goes to seek females, and leads them one by one to lay in the retreat he has built. Then he remains in the neighbourhood until the young come out, ready to throw himself furiously with his spines on any imprudent intruders.

*Dwellings woven with greater art.*—Without doubt the class of Birds furnishes the most expert artisans in the industry of the woven dwelling. In our own country we may see them seeking every day to right and left, carrying a morsel of straw, a pinch of moss, a hair from a horse's tail, or a tuft of wool caught in a bush. They intermingle these materials, making the framework of the construction with the coarser pieces, keeping those that are warmer and more delicate for the interior. These nests, attached to a fork in a branch or in a shrub, hidden in the depth of a thicket, are little masterpieces of skill and patience. To describe every form and every method would fill a volume. But I cannot pass in silence those which reveal a science sure of itself, and which are not very inferior to what man can do in this line. The Lithuanian Titmouse (*Ægithalus pendulinus*), whose

FIG. 26.

works have been well described by Baldamus, lives in the marshes in the midst of reeds and willows in Poland, Galicia, and Hungary. Its nest, which resembles none met in our own country, is always suspended above the water, two or three metres above the surface, fixed to a willow branch.[1] All individuals do not exhibit the same skill in fabricating their dwelling; some are more careful and clever than others who are less experienced. Some also are obliged by circumstances to hasten their work. It frequently happens that Magpies spoil or even altogether destroy with blows of their beaks one of these pretty nests. The unfortunate couple are obliged to recommence their task, and if this accident happens two or three times to the same household, it can easily be imagined that, discouraged and depressed by the advancing season, they hasten to build a shelter anyhow, only doing what is indispensable, and neglecting perfection. However this may be, the nests which are properly finished have the form of a purse, twenty centimetres high and twelve broad. (Fig. 27.) At the side an opening, prolonged by a passage which is generally horizontal, gives access to the interior. Sometimes another opening is found without any passage. Every nest in the course of construction possessed this second entry, but it is usually filled up when the work is completed. When the bird has resolved to establish its retreat, it first chooses a hanging branch presenting bifurcations which can be utilised as a rigid frame on which to weave the lateral walls of the habitation. It intercrosses wool and goat's hair so as to form two courses which are afterwards united to each other below, and

[1] Baldamus, *Beiträge zur Oologie und Nidologie*, 1853, pp. 419-445.

FIG. 27.

constitute the first sketch of the nest, at this moment like a flat-bottomed basket. This is only the beginning. The whole wall is reinforced by the addition of new material. The architect piles up down from the poplar and the willow, and binds it all together with filaments torn from the bark of trees, so as to make a whole which is very resistant. Then a couch is formed by heaping up wool and down at the bottom of the nest.

The American Baltimore Oriole, also called the Baltimore Bird, is a distinguished weaver. With strong stalks and hemp or flax, fastened round two forked twigs corresponding to the proposed width of nest, it makes a very delicate sort of mat, weaving into it quantities of loose tow. The form of the nest might be compared to that of a ham; it is attached by the narrow portion to a small branch, the large part being below. An opening exists at the lower end of the dwelling, and the interior is carefully lined with soft substances, well interwoven with the outward netting, and it is finished with an external layer of horse-hair, while the whole is protected from sun and rain by a natural canopy of leaves.

The Rufous-necked Weaver Bird, as described by Brehm, shows itself equally clever. Its nest is woven with extreme delicacy, and resembles a long-necked decanter hung up with the opening below. From the bottom of the decanter a strong band attaches the whole to the branch of a tree. (Fig. 28.) The Yellow Weaver Bird of Java, as described by Forbes, constructs very similar retort-shaped nests.[1]

These birds have no monopoly of these careful

1 H. O. Forbes, *A Naturalist's Wanderings in the Eastern Archipelago*, 1885, pp. 56-58.

dwellings; a considerable number of genera have carried this industry to the same degree of perfection.

When animals apply themselves in association to any work, they nearly always exhibit in it a marked superiority over neighbouring species among whom the individuals work in isolation. The construction of

FIG. 28.

dwellings is no exception, and the nests of the Sociable Weaver Birds of South Africa are the best constructed that can be found. These birds live together in considerable colonies; the members of an association are at least two hundred in number, and sometimes rise to five hundred. The city which they construct is a marvel of industry. They first make with grass a sloping roof, giving it the form of a mushroom or an open umbrella, and they place it in such a way that it is supported by the trunk of a tree and one or two

FIG. 29.

of the branches. (Fig. 29) This thatch is prepared with so much care that it is absolutely impenetrable to water. Beneath this protecting shelter each couple constructs its private dwelling. All the individual nests have their openings below, and they are so closely pressed against one another that on looking at the construction from beneath, the divisions cannot be seen. One only perceives a surface riddled with holes like a skimmer; each of these holes is the door of a nest. The work may endure for several years; as long as there is room beneath the roof the young form pairs near their cradle; but at last, as the colony continues to increase, a portion emigrate to found a new town on another tree in the forest.[1]

The industry of the woven dwelling does not flourish among mammals; but there is one which excels in it. This is the Dwarf Mouse (*Mus minutus*), certainly one of the smallest Rodents. It generally lives amidst reeds and rushes, and it is perhaps this circumstance which has impelled it to construct an aërial dwelling for its young, not being able to deposit them on the damp and often flooded soil. This retreat is not used in every season; its sole object is for bringing forth the young. It is therefore a genuine nest, not only by the manner in which it is made, but by the object it is intended to serve. The mouse chooses in the midst of its usual domain a tuft with leaves more or less crossed; but not too inextricable, so that there may remain in the midst an empty space, in the centre of which the work will be arranged. Great ingenuity is shown in the preliminaries; the mouse simplifies its task by utilising material within its reach instead of going afar to collect them with trouble. The little animal examines the thicket, and on reflection chooses some

[1] An early description of this bird is to be found in W. Paterson's *Narrative of Four Journeys into the Country of the Hottentots*, 1789; also in Le Vaillant's *Second Voyage dans l'intérieur de l'Afrique*, 1803, t. iii., p. 322.

thirty leaves which appear suitable. Then, without detaching them, it tears each into seven or eight threads which are held together by the base, and remain attached to the reeds. It is a clever idea to

FIG. 30.

avoid losing a natural point of support. The little bands being thus prepared, they are interlaced and crossed with much art, the animal comes and goes, placing first one of them, then another above, taken from a different leaf. It has soon woven a ball about the size of the fist, and hollowed out the interior. (Fig. 30.) Delicate materials are not lacking around to make a soft bed. The mouse gleans and constantly brings in the light down of the willow, grains with cottony crests, and the petals of flowers. This is all carefully fitted, and when the edifice is completed the female retires into it to bring forth her young, which are there well sheltered against the dangers without, and the caprices of storms and floods. The nest is made with as much delicacy as that of any bird, and no other mammal except Man is capable of executing such weaver's work.

*The art of sewing among birds.*—There are birds which have succeeded in solving a remarkable difficulty. Sewing seems so ingenious an art that it must be reserved for the human species alone. Yet the Tailor Bird, the *Orthotomus longicauda*, and other species possess the elements of it. They place their nests in a large leaf which they prepare to this end. With their beaks they pierce two rows of holes along the two edges of the leaf; they then pass a stout thread from one side to the other alternately. With this leaf, at first flat, they form a horn in which they weave their nest with cotton or hair. (Fig. 31.) These labours of weaving and sewing are preceded by the spinning of the thread. The bird makes it itself by twisting in its beak spiders' webs, bits of cotton, and little ends of wool. Sykes found that the threads used for sewing were knotted at the ends.[1] It is impossible not to admire animals who have skilfully triumphed over all the obstacles met with in the course of these complicated operations.[2]

[1] *Catalogue of Birds, etc.*, p. 16.

[2] Tristram, "On the Ornithology of Northern Africa," *Isis*, 1859-60.

Certain Spiders, while they do not actually sew in the sense that they perforate the leaves

FIG. 31.

they use to build their nest, and draw the thread through them, yet subject the leaves to an operation which cannot well be called anything else but sewing it.[1]

*Modifications of dwellings according to season and climate.*—A certain number of facts show that these various industries are not fixed and immutable instincts imposed on the species. Certain Birds change the form of their dwelling according to the climate, or according to the season in which they inhabit it. For example, the Crossbill, *Loxia tænioptera* (Fig. 32), does not build its nest according to the same rules in Sweden as in France. It builds in every season. The winter shelter is spherical, constructed with very dry lichens, and it is very large. A very narrow opening, just sufficient for the passage of the owner, prevents the external cold from penetrating within. The summer nests are much smaller, in consequence of a reduction in the thickness of the walls. There is no longer need to fear that the cold will come through them, and the animal gives itself no superfluous trouble.

Again, the Baltimore Oriole, which inhabits both the Northern and Southern States of North America, knows very well how to adapt his manner of work to the external circumstances in which he lives. Thus, in the Southern States the nest is woven of delicate materials united in a rather loose fashion, so that the air can circulate freely and keep the interior fresh; it is lined with no warm substance, and the entrance is turned to the west so that the sun only sends into it the oblique evening rays. In the north, on the contrary, the nest is oriented to the south to profit by all the warm sunshine; the walls are thick, without

[1] McCook describes, and gives good illustrations of, these nests in various stages of progress, *American Spiders*, vol. i. p. 302.

interstices, and the dwelling is carpeted in the warmest and softest manner. Even in the same region there is great diversity in the style, neatness, and finish of the nests, as well as in the materials used. Skeins of silk and hanks of thread have frequently been found in the Baltimore Bird's nest, so woven up and entangled that they could not be withdrawn. As such materials could not be obtained before the introduction of Europeans, it is evident that this bird, with the sagacity of a good architect, knows how to select the strongest and best materials for his work. Many other facts might be quoted, but these suffice to show that the species is not animated by an inevitable instinct, but that each individual, skilful no doubt by heredity, can modify the

FIG. 32.

methods transmitted to him by his ancestors, according to his own experience and his own judgment.

*Built dwellings.*—The built dwelling, the expression of the highest civilisation, still remains to be studied. Man has only known how to construct this kind of shelter at a comparatively late period in his evolution; and among animals we do not find it widely spread, much less so, certainly, than the two foregoing methods, especially the first. The difficulty of this work is greater, and it only arrives at considerable development among very sociable species, since the united efforts of a great number of individuals are needed to carry it on.

There are, however, masons who operate separately; but their constructions are rudimentary. The characteristic of all these works is that they are manufactured with some substance to which the animal gives a determined form while it is still soft, and that in drying it preserves this form and acquires solidity. The matter most usually employed is softened and tempered earth—mortar; but there are animals who use with success more delicate bodies. Two examples will suffice to indicate the nature of these exceptions: the labours of Wasps and those of certain Swallows.

*Paper nests.*—Certain Wasps, by the material of their dwellings, approach the Japanese; they build with paper. This paper or cardboard is very strong and supplies a solid support; moreover, being a bad conductor of heat, it contributes to maintain an equable temperature within the nest. The constructions of these insects, though they do not exhibit the geometric arrangement of those of Bees, are not less interesting. The paper which they employ is manufactured on the spot, as the walls of the cells

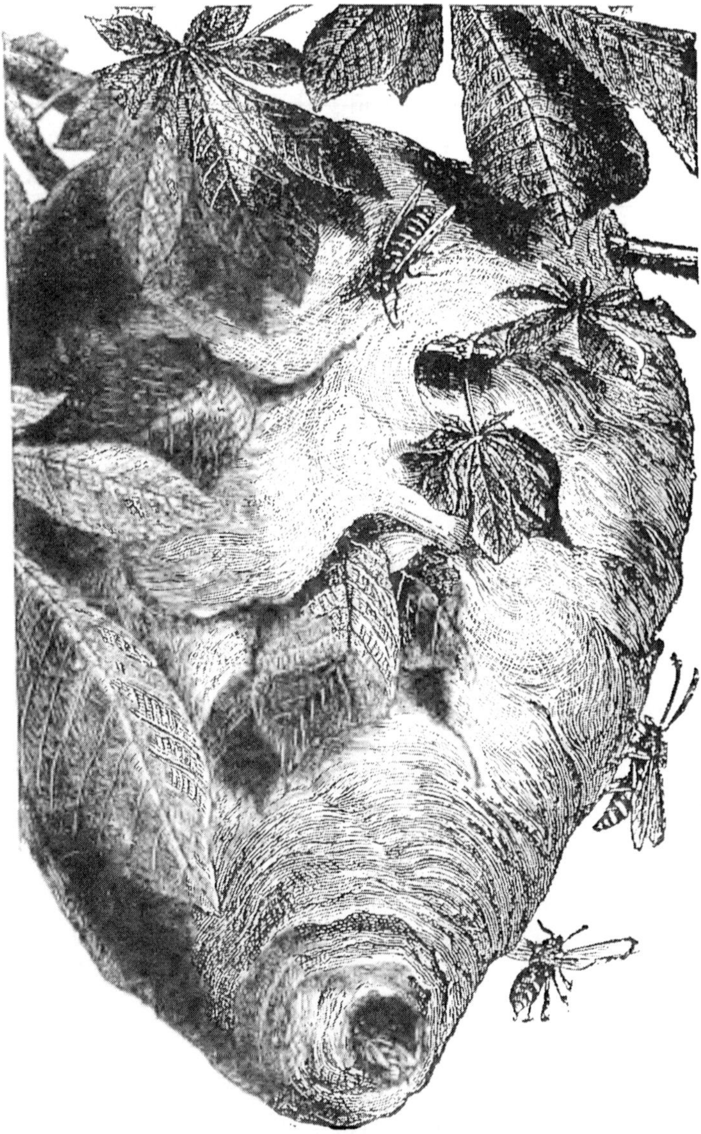

FIG. 33.

develop. Detritus of every kind enters into its preparation: small fragments of wood, sawdust, etc.; anything is good. These Hymenoptera possess no organ specially adapted to aid them; it is with their saliva that they glue this dust together and make of it a substance very suitable for its purpose. The dwellings often reach considerable size, yet they are always begun by a single female, who does all the work without help until the moment when the first eggs come out; she is thus furnished with workers capable of taking a share in her task. The *Vespa sylvestris* builds a paper nest of this kind, hanging to the branch of a tree, like a great grey sphere prolonged to a blunt neck. (Fig. 33.) The Hornet's nest is similar in construction.

*Gelatine nests.*—These are made by certain Swallows who nest in grottoes or cliffs on the edge of the sea. After having collected from the water a gelatinous substance formed either of the spawn of fish or the eggs of Mollusca, they carry this substance on to a perpendicular wall, and apply it to form an arc of a circle. This first deposit being dry, they increase it by sticking on to its edge a new deposit. Gradually the dwelling takes on the appearance of a cup and receives the workers' eggs. (Fig. 34.) These dwellings are the famous swallows' nests, so appreciated by the epicures of the extreme East, which are edible in the same way as, for example, caviare.

*Constructions built of earth—Solitary masons.*—Certain animals, whose dwelling participates in the nature of a hollow cavern, make additions to it which claim a place among the constructions with which we are now occupied.

The *Anthophora parietina* is in this group; it is

a small bee which lives in liberty in our climate. As its name indicates, it prefers to frequent the walls of old buildings and finds a refuge in the interstices, hollowing out the mortar half disintegrated by time.

FIG. 34.

The entrance to the dwelling is protected by a tube curved towards the bottom, and making an external prominence. (Fig. 35.) The owner comes and goes by this passage, and as it is curved towards the earth

FIG. 35.

the interior is protected against a flow of rain, while at the same time the entry is rendered more difficult for *Melectes* and *Anthrax*. These insects, in fact, watch the departure of the *Anthophora* to endeavour to penetrate into their nests and lay their eggs there. The gallery of entry and exit has been built with grains of sand, the *débris* produced by the insect in working. These grains of sand glued together form, on drying, a very resistant wall.[1]

The other animals of which I have to speak are genuine masons, who prepare their mortar by tempering moistened earth. Every one has seen the Swallow in spring working at its nest in the corner of a window. It usually establishes its dwelling in an angle, so that the three existing walls can be utilised, and to have an enclosed space there is need only to add the face. It usually gives to this the form of a quarter of a sphere, and begins it by applying earth more or less mixed with chopped hay against the walls which are to support the edifice. At the summit of the construction a hole is left for entry and exit. During the whole of its sojourn in our country the Swallow uses this dwelling, and even returns to it for many years in succession, as long as its work will support the attacks of time. The faithful return of these birds to their old nest has been many times proved by attaching ribbons to their claws; they have always returned with the distinctive mark.

The *Chalicodoma*, whose name of Mason Bee indicates the industry it exercises, is a hymenopterous relative to our Bees, long since carefully studied by Réaumur. It does not live in societies like the latter,

[1] Latreille, "Observations sur l'abeille parietine (*Anthophora parietina*)," *Annales du Muséum d'Hist. Nat.*, t. iii., 1804, p. 257.

and exhibits individual initiative and skill as great as the swallows. The females accomplish the work which I am about to describe. The little cells which they build are arranged, to the number of eight or ten together, in the most various places; sometimes on a pebble, sometimes on a branch, or, again, on a stone wall. (Fig. 36.) The insect collects earth as fine as possible, such as the dust of a trodden path, and tempers it with its own saliva. It places side

FIG. 36.

by side these little balls of mortar and the work soon takes the form of a cupola, to the edge of which it constantly adds new deposits. The sun quickly dries the hole and gives it the necessary consistence. When the cell has acquired sufficient height, the *Chalicodoma* abandons its occupation of mason, and visits flowers for pollen and nectar wherewith to fill the little chamber. It goes back to the nest, disgorges its supply, and returns to the field, until the little cup of earth is full to the edge. When the dwelling is thus prepared and provisioned, the insect lays an egg there and closes the upper part with a vault, built by successive deposits over the opening, which is more and more narrowed until it is finally shut up. Having completed a chamber, it passes on to the next, and so on until it has assured the fate of all its descendants.

This hymenopterous insect certainly shows in its acts as an artisan an inevitable instinct: hereditary intelligence has become less personal and less spontaneous. In certain cases, however, the instinct loses its rigidity and automatism. Thus, when a *Chalicodoma*, at the moment of preparing to accomplish its task, finds an old nest, still capable of repair although dilapidated, it does not hesitate to take possession of it and to silence its assumed innate instinct of building. It profits by the work already done, and is content to fill up the cracks or to re-establish the masonry where defective; then it provisions the renewed cells with honey, and lays its eggs in them. In certain circumstances it shows itself still more sparing of trouble, and boldly rebels against the law which seems to be imposed on it by nature. If it feels itself sufficiently strong, the *Chalicodoma* throws itself on one of its fellows, a peaceful constructor that has almost completed its work; it chases it away, and takes possession of its property to shelter its own eggs. Instead of manufacturing the cell from bottom to top, it has only to complete it. Such acts evidently show the reflection appearing through instinct.

Besides the Swallows, of which I have already spoken, birds offer us several types of skilful construction with tempered earth.

The Flamingo, which lives in marshes, cannot place its eggs on the earth nor in the trunks of trees, which are often absent from its domain. It builds a cone of mud, which dries and becomes very resistant, and it prepares at the summit an excavation open to the air; this is the nest. The female broods by sitting with her legs hanging over the sides of the hillock on which her little family prospers above the waters and the damp soil.

A Perch in the Danube also manufactures a dwelling of dried earth. It gives it the form of an elliptic cupola, and prepares a semicircular opening for entry and exit.

The bird which shows itself the most skilful mason is probably the Oven-Bird (*Furnarius rufus*) of Brazil and La Plata. Its name is owing to the form of the nest which it constructs for brooding, and which has the appearance of an oven. It is very skilful and knows how to build a dome of clay without scaffolding, which is not altogether easy. Having chosen for the site of its labours a large horizontal branch, it brings to it a number of little clay balls more or less combined with vegetable *débris*, works them altogether, and makes a very uniform floor, which is to serve as a platform for the rest of the work. When this is done, and while the foundation is drying, the bird arranges on it a circular border of mortar slightly inclined outwards. This becomes hard; it raises it by a new application, this time inclined inwards. All the other layers which will be placed above this will also be inclined towards the interior of the chamber. As the structure rises, the circle which terminates it above becomes more and more narrow. Soon it is quite small, and the animal, closing it with a little ball of clay, finds itself in possession of a well-made dome. Naturally it prepares an entrance; the form of this is semicircular. But this is not all. In the interior it arranges two partitions: one vertical, the other horizontal, separating off a small chamber. The vertical partition begins at one of the edges of the door, so that the air from without cannot penetrate directly into the dwelling, which is thus protected against extreme variations of temperature. It is in the compartment thus formed that the female lays her eggs and broods, after having taken care to carpet it with a thick layer of small herbs.

"In favourable seasons, the Oven-birds begin building in the autumn," Hudson tells us, "and the work is resumed during the winter whenever there is a spell of mild, wet weather. Some of their structures are finished early in winter, others not until spring, everything depending on the weather and the condition of the birds. In cold, dry weather, and when food is scarce, they do not work at all. The site chosen is a stout horizontal branch, or the top of a post, and they also frequently build on a cornice or the roof of a house; and sometimes, but rarely, on the ground. The material used is mud, with the addition of horse hair or slender fibrous rootlets, which make the structure harder and prevent it from cracking. I have frequently seen a bird engaged in building first pick up a thread or hair, then repair to a puddle, where it was worked into a pellet of mud about the size of a filbert, then carried to the nest. When finished the structure is shaped outwardly like a baker's oven, only with a deeper and narrower entrance. It is always placed very conspicuously, and with the entrance facing a building, if one be near, or if at a roadside it looks towards the road; the reason for this being, no doubt, that the bird keeps a continuous eye on the movements of people near it while building, and so leaves the nest opened and unfinished on that side until the last, and then the entrance is necessarily formed. When the structure has assumed the globular form with only a narrow opening, the wall on one side is curved inwards, reaching from the floor to the dome, and at the inner extremity an aperture is left to admit the bird to the interior or second chamber, in which the eggs are laid. A man's hand fits easily into the first or entrance chamber, but cannot be twisted about so as to reach the eggs in the interior cavity, the entrance being so small and high up. The interior is lined with dry soft grass, and five white pear-shaped eggs are laid. The oven is a foot or more in diameter, and is sometimes very massive, weighing eight or nine pounds, and so strong that, unless loosened by the swaying of the branch, it often remains unharmed for two or three years. A new oven is built every year, and I have more than once seen a second oven built on the top of the first, when this has been placed very advantageously, as on a projection and against a wall." [1]

*Masons working in association.*—Ants have already furnished us with numerous proofs of their intelligence and their prodigious industry. So remote from Man from the anatomical point of view, they are of all animals those whose psychic faculties bring them nearest to him. Sociable like him, they have under-

[1] P. L. Sclater and W. H. Hudson, *Argentine Ornithology*, 1888, vol. i. pp. 168, 169. See also Burmeister, "Ueber die Eier und Nester einiger brasilianischen Vögel," *Cabani's Journal für Ornith.*, 1853, pp. 161-177.

gone an evolution parallel to his which has placed them at the head of Insects in the same way as he has become superior to all other Mammals. The brain in Ants as in Man has undergone a disproportionate development. Like Man, they possess a language which enables them to combine their efforts, and there is no human industry in which these insects have not arrived at a high degree of perfection. If in certain parts of the earth human societies are superior to those of Ants, in many others the civilisation of Ants is notably superior. No village of Kaffirs can be compared to a palace of the Termites. The classifications separate these insects (sometimes called "White Ants") from the Ants, since the latter are Hymenoptera, while the former are ranked among the Neuroptera, but their constructions are almost alike, and may be described together. These small animals, relatively to their size, build on a colossal scale compared to Man; even our most exceptional monuments cannot be placed beside their ordinary buildings. (Fig. 37.) The domes of triturated and plastered clay which cover their nests may rise to a height of five metres; that is to say, to dimensions equal to one thousand times the length of the worker. The Eiffel Tower, the most elevated monument of which human industry can boast, is only one hundred and eighty-seven times the average height of the worker. It is three hundred metres high, but to equal the Termites' audacity, it would have to attain a height of 1,600 metres.

The different species of Termite are not equally industrious. The *T. bellicosus* seems to have carried the art of construction to the highest point. All the individuals of the species are not alike; there exists

FIG. 37.

a polymorphism which produces creatures of three sorts: 1, the *soldiers*, recognised by their large heads and long sharp mandibles, moved by powerful muscles; it is their mission to defend the whole colony against its adversaries, and the wounds they can produce, fatal to creatures of their own size, are painful even to man; 2, the *workers*, who labour as navvies and architects, and take charge of the pupæ: they form the great majority of the community; 3, the *king* and *queen*. (Fig. 38.) To each nest there is

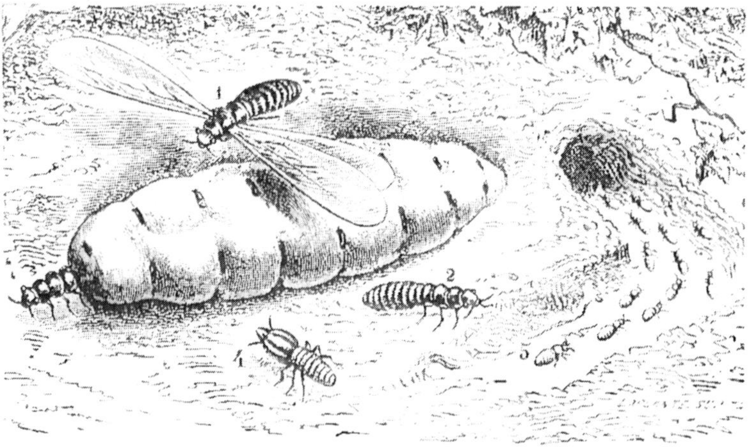

FIG. 38.

1. King before wings are cast off; 2. Worker (neuter); 3. Queen with abdomen distended with eggs; 4. Soldier (neuter); 5. Young (resembling adults).

usually only a single fertile and lazy couple. These two personages do absolutely nothing; the soldiers and the workers care for them and bring them food. They have both possessed wings, but these fall off. The queen reigns but does not govern; she lays. The king is simply the husband of the queen. The internal administration of the palace is bound up with the parts played by these three kinds of beings.

The lofty nest, or Termitarium, constitutes a hillock in the form of a cupola. The interior arrangement is very complicated, and at the same time very well adapted to the life of the inhabitants. There are four storeys in all, covered by the general exterior walls. (Fig. 39.) The walls of the dome are very thick; at the base they measure from sixty to eighty centimetres.

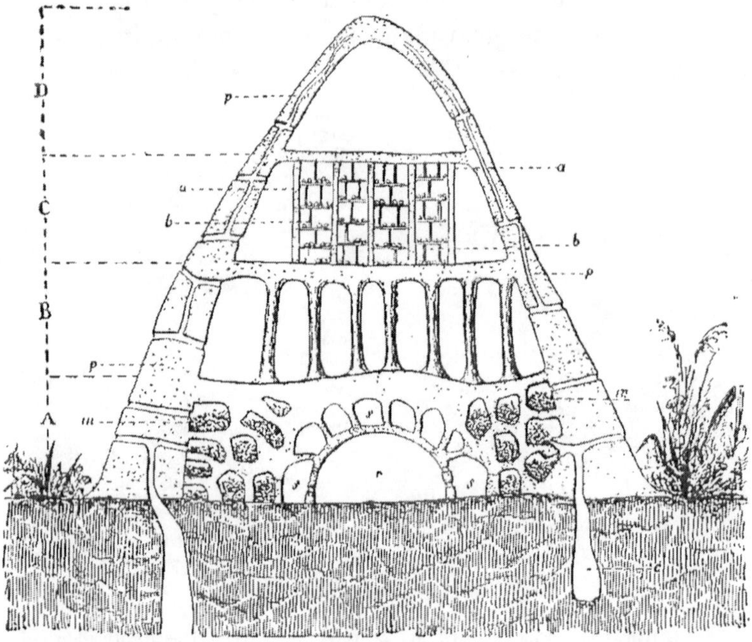


FIG. 39.

The clay in drying attains the hardness of brick, and the whole is very coherent. The sentinels of herds of wild cattle choose these tumuli as observatories and do not break them down. The walls of this exterior *enceinte* are hollowed by galleries of two kinds: some horizontal and giving access from outside to all the storeys; the others mounting spirally in the thickness of the wall to the summit of the dome. When the colony is in full activity, after the construction is completed, these little passages have no further use. They served for the passage of the masons when building the cupola; and they could be utilised again if a breach should be made in the wall. At the lower part these galleries in the wall are very wide, and they sink into the earth beneath the palace to a depth of more than 1 metre 50.

These subterranean passages (*c*) are the catacombs of the Termites, and have a very close analogy with those of old and populous human cities. Their origin is similar; they are ancient quarries. The insects hollowed them in obtaining the necessary clay for their labours. Later, when the rains come, they serve as drains to carry off the water which might threaten to invade the dwelling.

Such is the external wall within which a busy population swarms. On passing to the interior let us first enter the ground-floor. In the centre is found the royal chamber (*r*). The walls are extremely strong and are supplied with windows for ventilation, and with doors to enable the Termites to render their services. It is necessary to renew the air in this chamber, which constantly contains more than two thousand insects. The openings are large enough for the passage of the workers, but the queen cannot pass through them. She is therefore a prisoner, as immured as a goddess in her temple. The chain which holds her is the prodigious development of her abdomen. As a virgin she could enter, when fertilised she cannot henceforth go out. She continuously elaborates eggs; every moment one appears at the orifice of the oviduct. The king remains near her, to give his assistance when occasion arises; hence he has received the title, absolutely justified under the circumstances, of Father of the People. Around the couple zealous attendants crowd. There are about two thousand of them, workers and soldiers, licking the two royal captives to remove any dust from their hairs, and bringing them food. As soon as the queen lays an egg, one of the workers hastens to take it gently between its jaws; it is the property of the state, and is carefully carried off to the second storey where the state nursery is situated.

The centre of the ground-floor, therefore, is occupied by the royal apartment; around this, and communicating with it by means of numerous entrances, are a number of cells used by the attendants on the queen (*s*). These little chambers are surrounded by a labyrinth of passages. The central room and its dependencies constitute a solid mass, around which other chambers are grouped. The whole space between it and the general wall is filled by vast storehouses, divided into many very spacious compartments. Within them are piled up the provisions which the Termites harvest every day; they consist especially of gums and the juices of plants, dried and pulverised so as to form a fine powder. Access to this property is given by means of large corridors which cross one another, and conduct to the outside through the horizontal galleries traversing the wall.

Above the whole of this ground-floor rests a thick vault of clay, which forms a strong floor for the first storey (B). This is composed of only a single room; it is put to no use, unless to isolate and support the apartments of the second floor, in the arrangement of which great care is exercised. There are no partitions on this floor, nothing but massive columns of clay to support the ceiling. These columns are more than a metre in height. It is a gigantic cathedral in which the liliputian architects have displayed considerable art. By means of this immense empty chamber a huge reservoir of air is placed in the very centre of the construction; through the galleries in the external wall it is sufficiently renewed for the purposes of respiration without too great a change in temperature.

The second storey rests on the first. To this the eggs are brought, and here the larvæ go through their evolution. Partitions of clay divide the space into a few large halls (*a*); these are again subdivided, this time not by earth, which is employed throughout the rest of the building, but by materials of a more delicate kind, which are, moreover, very bad conductors of heat (*b*). It is a question, in fact, of maintaining these little chambers at an almost constant temperature, favourable for the development of the eggs. The substances utilised for this purpose are fragments of wood and of gum. The Termites glue them together and thus form the walls of these important cells.

The arrangement of the top storey (D) is also disposed with a view of protecting the young who are the future of the city. It constitutes the attic, situated just beneath the cupola, and contains absolutely nothing; it simply serves to interpose beneath the summit of the edifice and the storey below a layer of air, which is a bad conductor of heat. The chamber devoted to the young is thus placed between two gaseous layers, a precaution which, combined with the choice of material, places it in the very best conditions for protection against the alternation of cold at night and torrid heat during the day.

It is difficult to know which to admire most—the audacity and vastness of the labour undertaken by these insects, or the ingenious foresight by which they ensure to their delicate larvæ a comfortable youth. There can be no doubt that these animals show themselves very superior to Man, taking into consideration his enormous size compared to theirs, in the art of building. Pillars, cupolas, vaults—nothing is too difficult or too complicated for these small and patient labourers.[1]

The Ants of our own lands do not yield to the Termites in this industry, and their dwellings are models of architecture. As they have been more carefully studied we know more exactly how they work, and the considerable sum of intelligence and initiative which they reveal in the accomplishment of their task. At the foot of hedges, on the outskirts of woods, they raise their frail monuments. The species are not equally skilful, and such differences as we have found in other industries may also be found here. In a general manner it was soon found that Ants do not, like Bees, obey a rigid instinct which

1 The earliest comprehensive account of the Termites and their industries was by Smeathman in the *Philosophical Transactions of the Royal Society*, vol. lxxi., 1781, pp. 139-192. Later they were studied by Lespès: "Recherches sur l'organisation et les mœurs du Termite lucifuge," *Ann. des Sci. Nat.*, 4me Série, t. v., fasc. 4 and 5, Paris, 1856. For a description of the South American Termitarium see also Bates's *Naturalist on the Amazons* (unabridged edition, 1892), pp. 208-214; and for the African Termites of Victoria Nyanza, a chapter in H. Drummond's *Tropical Africa*, 1888, pp. 123-158; while Forbes has briefly described them in Java, *Naturalist's Wanderings in the Eastern Archipelago*, pp. 73, 74.

ordains the line of conduct under every circumstance, and impels each individual to act so that his efforts are naturally combined and harmonised with those of his neighbours in the workshop. One soon perceives when observing an ant-hill that any individual insect follows, when working, a personal idea which it has conceived, and which it realises without troubling itself about the others. Often these latter are executing a quite contradictory plan. It is rather an anarchistic republic. Happily Ants are not obstinate, and when they see the idea of one of them disengaging itself from the labour commenced, they are content to abandon their own less satisfactory idea and to collaborate in the other's work. They are able, for the rest, to concert plans; the movements of their antennæ are a very complicated language containing many expressions, and the worker who desires the acceptance of his own point of view is not sparing in their use.[1] It sometimes happens that his efforts are vain, and that his companions manœuvre to thwart his schemes. In the presence of such resistance those who are determined to obtain the adoption of their own plans destroy the labours of their opponents; fierce struggles ensue, and here it is the strongest who becomes the architect-general.

The *Formica fusca* constructs its nest of plastered earth. The different superimposed storeys have been added one by one to the upper part of the old dwelling when the latter became too small for the

[1] For a discussion of the methods of communication among Ants, tending to the conclusion that these methods "almost amount to language," see Lubbock's *Ants, Bees, and Wasps*, chap. vi. And for a general discussion of language among animals, see Alix, *L'esprit de nos Bêtes*, pp. 331-367.

growing colony. In opening an ant-hill, they are found to be quite distinct from each other; each is divided by a large number of partitions into vaulted compartments. In the larger ones pillars of earth support the ceiling. The rooms communicate with one another by means of bull's-eye passages formed in the separating walls. The whole is small, proportioned to the size of the works, but excellently arranged.

When, in the council of the republic, it has been resolved to raise a common habitation, the workers operate in a singular manner. All the ants scatter themselves abroad, and with extreme activity take fragments of earth between their mandibles and place them on the summit of the dwelling. After some time the result of this microscopical work appears. The ancient roof, strengthened by all this material, becomes a thick terrace which the insects first cover very evenly. The earth, having been brought in grain by grain, is soft and easy to dig. The construction of the new storey begins at first by the hollowing out of a number of trenches. The ants scrape away in places the terrace which they have just made. They thus diminish the thickness of the layer at the spots where rooms, corridors, etc., are to be formed, and with the material thus obtained they form walls, partitions, and pillars. Soon the entire plan of the new storey may be perceived. It differs essentially from that which Man would adopt; in the latter case the walls would be shown by the hollowing out of the foundations; the work of these Hymenoptera, on the contrary, shows them in relief. These first arrangements made, the six-footed architects have only to complete their constructions by new deposits from without. Gradually the storey reaches a sufficient height. It remains to cover it, and this is not the easiest part of the business. The ceiling is formed of vaults going from one wall to another, or from a wall to a column. When one of these vaults is to be small, some millimetres at the most, the *Formica fusca* constructs it with the help of two ledges, which are made facing each other on the tops of two partitions. These prominences, formed of materials glued together by saliva, are enlarged by additions to their free edges. They advance to meet each other and soon join; it is wonderful to see each insect, following its individual initiative, profit by every twig or fragment capable of bearing any weight, in order to enlarge the overhanging ledges.

*Individual skill and reflection.*—This personality in work, which reveals the intelligent effort of each, has certainly its inconveniences for the common work. Badly-concerted operations may not succeed, and Huber witnessed an accident due to this cause.[1] Two walls facing each other were to be united by an arch. A foolish worker had begun to form a horizontal ledge on the summit of one of the walls without paying attention to the fact that the other wall was very much higher. By continuing the project the ceiling would have come against the middle of the opposite ceiling instead of resting on its summit. Another ant passes, examines affairs with an intelligent air, and evidently considers that this sort of work is absurd. Without consideration for the *amour-propre* of its unskilful fellow-citizen, it demolishes its work, raises the wall that is too low, and re-makes the construction correctly in the presence

[1] *Recherches sur les Mœurs des Fourmis indigènes*, pp. 47, 48.

of the observer. If this incident reveals inconceivable thoughtlessness in one of the members of this serious republic, it also brings to light the judgment, reflection, and decision of which they are capable, as well as a freedom which cannot be found in the works of instinct.

This *Formica fusca* sometimes finds itself in the presence of other difficulties. It may happen that the hall to be roofed is too large and the arch too considerable to allow of the cohesion of the materials employed. The insects soon become aware of the existence of this embarrassing state of things and remedy it in various ways, either by hastily constructing pillars in the centre of the too large room, or by some other method. Ebrard describes an artifice he has seen employed, which shows to what an extent ants can quickly appreciate and take advantage of the most unforeseen circumstances.[1] A worker was labouring to cover a large cell; two prominences, parts of opposite walls, were advancing towards each other, but there was still a space of from twelve to fifteen millimetres between them, and it seemed no longer possible to burden the two sides without risking a general downfall. The little mason was much disturbed. A graminaceous plant was growing near. The ant seemed anxious to take advantage of it, for it went to it and climbed up the stalk. After having examined and devised, it set about curving it in the direction of the edifice. To attain this object, it placed a little mass of moist earth on the extremity of the leaf, and fixed it there. Under the influence of this weight flexion was produced, but only at the end. This could not satisfy the insect;

[1] Ebrard, *Études de Mœurs*, Genève, 1864, p. 3.

it became a question of decreasing the resistance at the base. The ant gnawed a little at this spot; the desired result was attained, and the whole length of the leaf became bent over the building in course of construction. To prevent it bending back, and to ensure its remaining adherent to the roof, the worker returned to the plant and placed earth between the sheath and the stalk. This time all difficulties were surmounted, and there was a solid scaffolding to support the materials for the roof.

Among the *Lasius niger* the independence of the workers is perhaps still greater; no doubt they do their best to concert their efforts, but they do not succeed so well as if an inevitable instinct impelled them. Notwithstanding the irregularities of the construction, it is possible to recognise in it a whole formed of hollowed, concentric half-spheres; they have been added one after the other to the surface to increase the dwelling. The interval between these clay spheres constitutes a storey, cut up by the partitions which divide it into chambers and communicating galleries; the roofs of the largest halls are supported by numerous pillars. (Fig. 40.)

These ants, as Huber has shown, are highly accomplished in the art of constructing a cupola. When they wish to increase their nest by a new layer, they take advantage of the first wet day, the rain serving to agglutinate and unite the materials. They operate in almost the same way as the *Formica fusca*, though exhibiting more skill and resource as architects; they know better how to calculate beforehand the number of pillars required in a hall of a determined size. As soon as the rain has given the signal for work, they spread themselves abroad and prepare a very thick terrace on the external surface of the dwelling which has become too small. They carry to it small balls of earth ground very fine by their jaws, and then lightly piled up so as to pulverise afresh; these are then spread over the construction with the anterior legs. Then, by hollowing out, the ants trace the plan of the new storey, leaving the walls, partitions, and columns in relief. After having raised these parts to a sufficient height, all work together to cover them with a general ceiling, each ant applying itself to one small corner of the work.

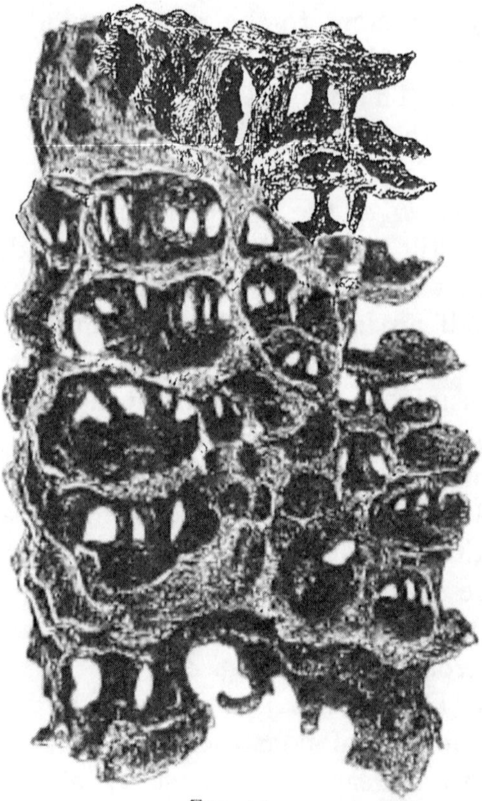

FIG. 40.

The vaulting is executed by the method already described; horizontal ledges, slanting from the summit of pillar or wall, are formed to meet one another. The insects are intelligent enough to begin their labour at the spots best fitted to give strong support to the overhanging materials, as for instance, at the angle of two walls. There is so much activity among the workers, and they are so anxious to take advantage of the damp, that the storey is sometimes completely finished in seven or eight hours. If the rain suddenly stops in the course of the work, they abandon operations, to complete them as soon as another shower falls.

I have already had occasion to speak of the covered passages and Aphis-pens built by Ants outside their dwellings. Besides these constructions, they also make roads in the fields, tearing up the grass and hollowing out the earth so as to form a beaten path free from the liliputian bushes in which there would be danger of becoming entangled, on returning to the nest laden with various and often embarrassing burdens.

Nor are Ants by any means alone in exhibiting the results of individual skill and reflection. It will, however, be sufficient to mention only one other example, that furnished by Spiders. McCook, in his great work, after elaborately describing and carefully illustrating the skill exhibited in individual cases by Spiders in their aërial labours, considers himself justified in concluding as follows:—"The manner in which the ends of the radii which terminate upon the herb are wrapped roundabout and braced by the notched zone; the manner in which the wide non-viscid scaffold lines are woven in order to give vantage ground from which to place the close-lying and permanent viscid spirals, upon which the usefulness of the orb depends—all these, to mention no other points, seem to indicate a very delicate perception of those modes (shall I also say principles?) of construction which are continually recognised in the art of the builder, the architect, and the engineer."[1]

[1] *American Spiders*, vol. i. p. 228.

*Dwellings built of hard materials united by mortar.*—Among mammals few animals have become so skilful in the art of building houses as the insects we have just been considering. There are, however, two who equal if they do not surpass them—the Musk-rat and its relative, the Beaver.

The Musk-rats of Canada live in colonies on the banks of streams or deep lakes, and construct dwellings which are very well arranged. In their methods we find combined the woven shelter with the house of built earth. Their cabins are established over the highest level of the water and look like little domes. In building them the animals begin by placing reeds in the earth; these they interlace and weave so as to form a sort of vertical mat. They plaster it externally with a layer of mud, which is mixed by means of the paws and smoothed by the tail. At the upper part of the hut the reeds are not pressed together or covered with earth, so that the air may be renewed in the interior. A dwelling of this kind, intended to house six or eight individuals who have combined to build it, may measure up to 65 centimetres in diameter. There is no door directly opening on to the ground. A subterranean gallery starts from the floor and opens out beneath the water. It presents secondary branches, some horizontal, through which the animal goes in search of roots for food, while others descend vertically to pits specially reserved for the disposal of ordure.

But it is, above all, the Beaver (*Castor fiber*) who exhibits the highest qualities as an engineer and mason. This industrious and sagacious Rodent is well adapted to inconvenience the partisans of instinct as an entity, apart from intelligence, which renders animals similar to machines and impels them to effect associated acts, without themselves being able to understand them, and with a fatality and determination from which they can under no circumstance escape.

Beavers now only live in Canada. A few individuals may, however, still be found on the banks of the lower Rhône, in Camargue, and on a few other European rivers. Several centuries ago they existed in the neighbourhood of Paris in considerable numbers. The Bièvre gained its name from the old French word for Beaver, and its resemblance to the English name, as well as to the German (*Biber*), is striking. In the sixteenth century, according to Bishop Magnus of Upsala, the Beaver was still common on the banks of the Rhine, the Danube, and on the shores of the Black Sea, and in the North it still exercised great art in its constructions. In the twelfth century it was found in Scotland and Wales. If we go back to ancient times, we find that Herodotus mentions that the Budini who lived in the neighbourhood of the Black Sea used the skins of the Beavers, which abounded there, on the borders of their garments; and in the time of Pliny the Beaver was so common there that he speaks of it as the Pontic Beaver. Fossil remains of the Beaver have also been found throughout Europe in conjunction with those of the Mammoth and other extinct animals.

But the civilisation of the Beaver has perished in the presence of Man's civilisation, or rather of his persecution. In regions where it is tracked and disturbed by Man the Beaver lives in couples, and is content to hollow out a burrow like the Otter's, instead of showing its consummate art. It merely vegetates,

15

fleeing from enemies who are too strong for it, and depriving itself of a dangerous comfort. But when the security of solitude permits these animals to unite in societies, and to possess, without too much fear, a pond or a stream, they then exhibit all their industry.

They build very well arranged dwellings, although at first sight they look like mere piles of twigs, branches, and logs, heaped in disorder on a small dome of mud. At the edge of a pond each raises his own lodge, and there is no work by the colony in common. If, however, there is a question of inhabiting the bank of a shallow stream, certain preliminary works become necessary. The rodents establish a dam, so that they may possess a large sheet of water which may be of fair depth, and above all constant, not at the mercy of the rise and fall of the stream. A sudden and excessive flood is the one danger likely to prove fatal to these dykes; but even our own constructions are threatened under such circumstances.

When the Beavers, tempted by abundance of willows and poplars, of which they eat the bark and utilise the wood in construction, have chosen a site, and have decided to establish a village on the edge of the water, there are several labours to be successively accomplished. Their first desire is to be in possession of a large number of felled trunks of trees. To obtain them they scatter themselves in the forest bordering the stream and attack saplings of from twenty to thirty centimetres in diameter. They are equipped for this purpose. With their powerful incisors, worked by strong jaws, they can soon gnaw through a tree of this size. But they are capable of attacking trees, even more than 100 cc. in circumference and some forty metres in height, with great skill and adaptability; "no better work could be accomplished by a most highly-finished steel cutting tool, wielded by a muscular human arm" (Martin). They operate seated on their hind quarters, and they make their incision in the wood with a feather edge. It was once supposed that they always take care so to direct their wood-cutting task that the tree may fall on the water-side, but this is by no means the case, and appears to be simply due, as Martin points out, to the fact that trees by the water-side usually slope towards the water. The austerity of labour alternates, it may be added, with the pleasures of the table. From time to time the Beavers remove the bark of the fallen trees, of which they are very fond, and feed on it.

Mr. Lewis H. Morgan studied the American Beaver with great care and thoroughness, more especially on the south-west shore of Lake Superior; he devotes fifty pages to the dams, and it is worth while to quote his preliminary remarks regarding them. "The dam is the principal structure of the beaver. It is also the most important of his erections as it is the most extensive, and because its production and preservation could only be accomplished by patient and long-continued labour. In point of time, also, it precedes the lodge, since the floor of the latter and the entrances to its chamber are constructed with reference to the level of the water in the pond. The object of the dam is the formation of an artificial pond, the principal use of which is the refuge it affords to them when assailed, and the water-connection it gives to their lodges and to their burrows in the banks. Hence, as the level of the pond must, in all cases, rise from one to two feet above these entrances for the protection of the animal from pursuit and capture, the surface-level of the pond must, to a greater or less extent, be subject to their immediate control. As the dam is not an absolute necessity to the beaver for the maintenance of his life, his normal habitation being rather natural ponds and rivers, and burrows in their banks, it is, in itself considered, a remarkable fact that he should have voluntarily transferred himself, by means of dams and ponds of his own construction, from a natural to an artificial mode of life.

"Some of these dams are so extensive as to forbid the supposition that they were the exclusive work of a single pair, or of a single family of beavers; but it does not follow, as has very generally been supposed, that several families, or a colony, unite for the joint construction of a dam. After careful examination of some hundreds of these structures, and of the lodges and burrows attached to many of them, I am altogether satisfied that the larger dams were not the joint-product of the labour of large numbers of beavers working together, and brought thus to immediate completion; but, on the contrary, that they arose from small beginnings, and were built upon year after year, until they finally reached that size which exhausted the capabilities of the location; after which they were maintained for centuries, at the ascertained standard, by constant repairs. So far as my observations have enabled me to form an opinion, I think they were usually, if not invariably, commenced by a single pair, or a single family of beavers; and that when, in the course of time, by the gradual increase of the dam, the pond had become sufficiently enlarged to accommodate more families than one, other families took up their residence upon it, and afterwards contributed by their labour to its maintenance. There is no satisfactory evidence that the American beavers either live or work in colonies; and if some such cases have been observed, it will either be found to be an exception to the general rule, or in consequence of the sudden destruction of a work upon the maintenance of which a number of families were at the time depending.

"The great age of the larger dams is shown by their size, by the large amount of solid materials they contain, and by the destruction of the primitive forest within the area of the ponds; and also by the extent of the beaver-meadows along the margins of the streams where dams are maintained, and by the hummocks formed upon them by and through the annual growth and decay of vegetation in separate hills. These meadows were undoubtedly covered with trees adapted to a wet soil when the dams were constructed. It must have required long periods of time to destroy every vestige of the ancient forest by the increased saturation of the earth, accompanied with occasional overflows from the streams. The evidence from these and other sources tends to show that these dams have existed in the same places for hundreds and thousands of years, and that they have been maintained by a system of continuous repairs.

"At the place selected for the construction of a dam, the ground is usually firm and often stony, and when across the channel of a flowing stream, a hard rather than a soft bottom is preferred. Such places are necessarily unfavourable for the insertion of stakes in the ground, if such were, in fact, their practice in building dams. The theory upon which beaver-dams are constructed is perfectly simple, and involves no such necessity. Soft earth, intermixed with vegetable fibre, is used to form an embankment, with sticks, brush, and poles embedded within these materials to bind them together, and to impart to them the requisite solidity to resist the effects both of pressure and of saturation. Small sticks and brush are used, in the first instance, with mud and earth and stones for down-weight. Consequently these dams are extremely rude at their commencement, and they do not attain their remarkably artistic appearance until after they have been raised to a considerable height, and have been maintained, by a system of annual repairs, for a number of years."[1]

There are two different kinds of beaver-dams, although they are both constructed on the same principle. One, the stick-dam, consists of interlaced stick and pole work below, with an embankment of earth raised with the same material upon the upper or water face. This is usually found in brooks or large streams with ill-defined banks. The other, the solid-bank dam, is not so common nor so interesting, and is usually found on those parts of the same stream where the banks are well defined, the channel deep, and the current uniform. In this kind the earth and mud entirely buries the sticks and poles, giving the whole a solid appearance. In the first kind the surplus water percolates through the dam along its entire length, while in the second it is discharged through a single opening in the crest formed for that purpose.

The materials being prepared in the manner I have previously described, the animals make ready to

[1] L. H. Morgan, *The American Beaver and his Works*, Philadelphia, 1868, pp. 82-86.

establish their dyke. They intermix their materials —driftwood, green willows, birch, poplars, etc.—in the bed of the river, with mud and stones, so making a solid bank, capable of resisting a great force of water; sometimes the trees will shoot up forming a hedge. The dam has a thickness of from three to four metres at the base, and about sixty centimetres at the upper part. The wall facing up-stream is sloping, that directed down-stream is vertical; this is the best arrangement for supporting the pressure of the mass of water which is thus expended on an inclined surface. In certain cases Beavers carry hydraulic science still further. If the course of the water is not very rapid, they generally make an almost straight dyke, perpendicular to the two banks, as this is then sufficient; but if the current is strong, they curve it so that the convexity is turned up-stream. In this way it is much better fitted to resist. Thus they do not always act in the same way, but arrange their actions so as to adapt them to the conditions of the environment.

The embankment being completed, the animals construct their lodges. Fragments of wood, deprived of the bark, are arranged and united by clay or mud which the Beavers take from the riverside, transport, mix, and work with their fore-paws. During a single night they can collect as much mud at their houses as amounts to some thousands of their small handfuls. They thus plaster their houses with mud every autumn; in the winter this freezes as hard as a stone and protects them from enemies. These cabins form domes from three to four metres in diameter at the base, and from two to two and a half metres in height. The floor is on a level with the surface of the artificial pond. A passage sinks in the earth and opens about one and a half metres below the level of the water, so that it cannot be closed up by ice during the severe winters of these regions.

Within, near the entry, the beavers form, with the aid of a partition, a special compartment to serve as a storehouse, and they there pile up enormous heaps of nenuphar roots as provisions for the days when ice and snow will prevent them from barking the young trunks.

A dwelling of this kind may last for three or four years, and the animal here tranquilly enjoys the fruits of its industry, as long as man fails to discover the retreat; for the beaver can escape by swimming from all carnivorous animals excepting, perhaps, the Otter. During floods the level of the water nearly reaches the hut; if the inundation is prolonged and the animal runs the risk of being asphyxiated beneath his dome, it breaks through the upper part with its teeth and escapes. When the water returns to its bed the beaver comes back, makes the necessary repairs, and resumes the usual peaceful course of its life.[1]

We have thus seen, from a shapeless hole to these complex dwellings, every possible stage; we have found among animals the rudiments of the different human habitations, certain animals, indeed, having arrived at a degree of civilisation which Man himself in some countries has not yet surpassed, or even indeed yet attained.

[1] The Beaver has been fully studied by Lewis H. Morgan, *The American Beaver*, 1868. See also Horace T. Martin's recent work, *Castorologia, or the History and Traditions of the Canadian Beaver*, 1892; in an appendix to this work will be found Samuel Hearne's classical account of the Beaver, written nearly two hundred years ago, and free from the many exaggerations and superstitions which have grown up around this animal.

# CHAPTER VII.

## THE DEFENCE AND SANITATION OF DWELLINGS.

GENERAL PRECAUTIONS AGAINST POSSIBLE DANGER—SEPARATION OF FEMALES WHILE BROODING—HYGIENIC MEASURES OF BEES—PRUDENCE OF BEES—FORTIFICATIONS OF BEES—PRECAUTIONS AGAINST INQUISITIVENESS—LIGHTING UP THE NESTS.

THE building of comfortable dwellings is not the last stage reached by the industry of animals. There are among them some who show genuine skill in rendering them healthy and defending them against invasions from without.

*General precautions against possible danger.*—Some animals show, even during the construction of the nest, extreme prudence in preventing its site from being discovered. Several authors refer to the stratagem of the Magpie, who begins several nests at the same time; but only one is intended to receive the brood, and that only is completed. The aim of the others is merely to distract attention. It is around these latter that the bird shows ostentatious activity, while it works at the real nest only for a few hours during the day, in the morning and evening.

The Crane takes equally ingenious precautions in order that its constant presence at the same spot may not arouse suspicion. It never comes or goes flying, but always on foot, concealing itself along tufts of reeds. De Homeyer even reports that the female at the time of laying covers her wings and back with mud. When dried this gives the animal a red tone, which causes it to be confused with neighbouring objects; this is intentional mimicry.

The Linnet (Fig. 41) again, wrongly accused of wanting judgment, is well aware that a pile of excrement at the foot of a tree announces a nest in the branches. It is careful to suppress this revealing sign, and every day takes it away in its beak to disperse it afar.

Birds will sometimes take the trouble to remove the eggs or the nest altogether, when the latter has been discovered, in order to avoid further risks of danger. The American Sparrow Hawk has been observed to do this, and the following incident is quoted by Bendire, from MacFarlane's *Manuscript Notes on Birds Nesting in British America*, concerning the Pigeon Hawk (*Falco columbarius*):—"On May 25, 1864, a trusty Indian in my employ found a nest placed in a thick branch of a pine tree at a height of about six feet from the ground. It was rather loosely constructed of a few dry sticks and a small quantity of coarse hay; it then contained two eggs; both parents were seen, fired at, and missed. On the 31st he revisited the nest, which still held but two eggs, and again missed the birds. Several days later he made another visit thereto, and, to his surprise, the eggs and parents had disappeared. His first impression was that some other person had taken them; but after looking carefully around he perceived both birds at a short distance, and this led him to institute a search which soon resulted in finding that the eggs must have been removed by the parent birds to the face of a muddy bank at least forty yards distant from the original nest. A few decayed leaves had been placed under them, but

FIG. 41.

nothing else in the way of lining. A third egg had been added in the interim. There can hardly be any doubt of the truth of the foregoing facts."[1]

[1] Bendire, *Life Histories of North American Birds*, 1892, p. 301.

*Separation of females while brooding.*—The Hornbill of Malacca[1] assures the protection of its nest and of the female while she is brooding in a singular manner. She lays in the hollow of a tree; as soon as she begins to sit on her eggs, the male closes the opening with diluted clay, only leaving a hole through which the captive can pass her beak to receive the fruits which he brings her in abundance. If the lady is thus cloistered as closely as in the most jealous harem, her lord and master at least expends on her the most attentive cares.

What can be the object of this strange custom? It has been asserted that during incubation the female loses her feathers and becomes unable to fly. The male would thus only wall her up as a precaution for fear of seeing her fall from the nest; because if this deplorable accident happened she would not be able to get back again. It seems to me that the effect is here taken for the cause, and that the falling off of feathers and torpidity must be the result rather than the motive of cloistration. One is tempted to believe that the male desires by this method to guarantee his female and her offspring against the attacks of squirrels or rapacious birds.

*Hygienic measures of Bees.*—Among the animals who expend industry on hygiene and the protection of their dwellings, we must place Bees in the first line. It may happen that mice, snakes, and moths may find their way into a hive. Assaulted by the swarm, and riddled with stings, they die without being able to escape. These great corpses cannot be dragged out by the Hymenoptera, and their putrefaction threatens

[1] Bernstein, "Ueber Nester und Eier einiger Javaschen Vögel," *Cabani's Journ. f. Ornith.*, 1859.

to cause disease. To remedy this scourge the insects immediately cover them with *propolis*—that is to say, the paste which they manufacture from the resin of poplars, birches, and pines. The corpse thus sheltered from contact with the air does not putrefy. In other respects Bees are very careful about the cleanliness of their dwellings; they remove with care and throw outside dust, mud, and sawdust which may be found there. Bees are careful also not to defile their hives with excrement, as Kirby noted; they go aside to expel their excretions, and in winter, when prevented by extreme cold or the closing of the hive from going out for this purpose, their bodies become so swollen from retention of fæces that when at last able to go out they fall to the ground and perish. Büchner records the observations of a friend of his during a season in which a severe epidemic of dysentery had broken out among the bees, which interfered with the usual habits of the insects; on careful examination of a hive it was found that a cavity in the posterior wall of the hive, containing crumbled clay, had been used as an earth closet. Many mammals are equally careful in this respect; thus, for example, the Beaver, as Hearne observed, always enters the water, or goes out on the ice, to urinate or defæcate; the fæces float and are soon disintegrated.

Animals are also careful about aëration. Thus, among Bees, in a hive full of very active insects the heat rises considerably and the air is vitiated. A service for aëration is organised. Bees ranged in files one above the other in the interior agitate their wings with a feverish movement; this movement causes a current of air which can be felt by holding the hand before the opening of the hive. When the workers of the corps are fatigued, comrades who have been resting come to take their place. These acts are not the result of a stupid instinct which the Hymenoptera obey without understanding. If we place a swarm, as Huber did, in a roomy position where there is plenty of air, they do not devote themselves to an aimless exercise. This only takes place in the narrow dwellings which Man grants to his winged guests.

The attention of Ants to public hygiene is more than equalled by their attention to personal hygiene. Without going into the question of their athletic exercises, which have attracted considerable attention, it is sufficient to quote one observer as to their habits of cleanliness. McCook remarks:—"The Agricultural Ants—and the remark applies to all other Ants of which I have knowledge—is one of the neatest of creatures in her personal habits. I think I have never seen one of my imprisoned harvesters, either *Barbatus* or *Crudelis*, in an untidy condition. They issue from their burrows, after the most active digging, even when the earth is damp, without being perceptibly soiled. Such minute particles of dust as cling to the body are carefully removed. Indeed, the whole body is frequently and thoroughly cleansed, a duty which is habitually, I might almost venture to say invariably, attended to after eating and after sleep. In this process the Ants assist one another; and it is an exceedingly interesting sight which is presented to the observer when this general 'washing up' is in progress."[1]

*Prudence of Bees.*—Certain species exhibit very great prudence, especially the *Melipona geniculata*,

[1] H. C. McCook, *Agricultural Ants of Texas*, 1879, chapter on "Toilet, Sleeping, and Funeral Habits," p. 125.

which lives in a wild state in South America. They place their combs in the hollow of a tree or the cleft of a rock; they fill up all the crevices and only leave a round hole for entry. And even this they are accustomed to close every evening by a small partition, which they remove in the morning. This door is shut with various materials, such as resin or even clay, which the bees bring on their legs as those of our own country bring pollen.

All these facts were observed with great exactness in a swarm given in 1874 by M. Drory (who during a long period of years studied every Brazilian species of *Melipona* at Bordeaux) to the Jardin d'Acclimatation. It was even seen that the door might be put up under certain circumstances in open day, as for example, when a storm or sudden cold delays the appearance of the workers. If one of them happened to be late it had to perforate the partition, and the hole was then stopped up again.

*Fortifications of Bees.*—As these facts take place always they may be called instinctive; but that is not the case with regard to defences elevated with a view to a particular circumstance, and which disappear when the danger to which they correspond disappears. Such are the labours of the bees to repel the invasions of the large nocturnal Death's-head Moth. (Fig. 42.) He is very greedy of honey, and furtively introduces himself into the hives. Protected by the long and fluffy hairs which cover him, he has little to fear from stings, and gorges himself with the greatest freedom on the stores of the swarm. Huber, in his admirable investigations,[1] narrates that one year in Switzerland numbers of hives were

[1] Huber, *Nouvelles observations sur les Abeilles.*

emptied, and contained no more honey in summer than in the spring. During that year Death's-head Moths were very numerous. The illustrious naturalist soon became certain that this moth was guilty of the

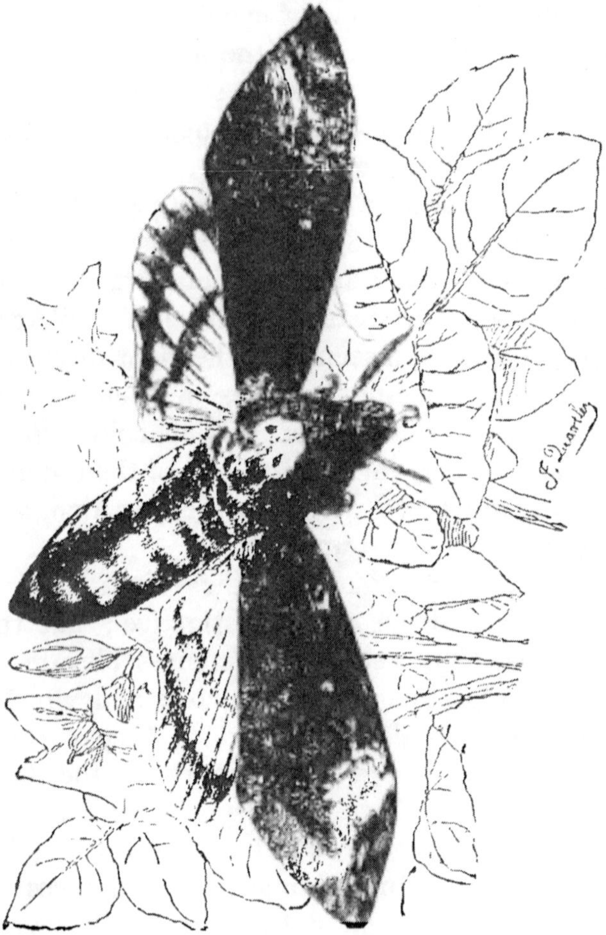

FIG. 42.

thefts in question. While he was reflecting as to what should be done, the bees, who were more directly interested, had invented several different methods of procedure. Some closed the entrance with wax, leaving only a narrow opening through which the great robber could not penetrate. Others built up before the opening a series of parallel walls, leaving between them a zigzag corridor through which the Hymenoptera themselves were able to enter. But the intruder was much too long to perform this exercise successfully. Man utilises defences of this kind; it is thus at the entrance of a field, for example, he places a turnstile, or parallel bars that do not face each other; the passage is not closed for him, but a cow is too long to overcome the obstacle. In years when the Death's-head Moth is rare the bees do not set up these barricades, which, indeed, they themselves find troublesome. For two or three consecutive years they leave their doors wide open. Then another invasion occurs, and they immediately close the openings. It cannot be denied that in these cases their acts agree with circumstances that are not habitual.[1]

*Precautions against inquisitiveness.*—I will finally quote a fact of defence which took place under circumstances that were absolutely exceptional, and which therefore exhibits genuine reflection in these insects. During the first exhibition of 1855 an artificial hive was set up, one face of which was closed by a glass pane. A wooden shutter concealed this pane, but passers-by opened it every moment to contemplate the work of the small insects. Annoyed by this inquisitiveness, the bees resolved to put an end to it, and cemented the shutter with *propolis.* When this substance dried it was no longer possible to open the shutter. The bees were visible to nobody.

*Lighting up the nests.*—An improvement of another

[1] These facts have recently been observed and recorded afresh by Mr. Clifford in *Nature Notes*, January 1893.

nature in the comfort of the dwelling is introduced by the *Baya*, and if the facts narrated are correct they are the most marvellous of all. It is a question of lighting up a nest by means of Glow-worms. The *Melicourvis baya* inhabits India ; it is a small bird related to the *Loxia*, already spoken of in this book. Like the latter it constructs a nest that is very well designed and executed. (Fig. 43.) It suspends it in general from a palm tree, but sometimes also from the roofs of houses. In these shelters, woven with extreme art, are always to be found little balls of dry and hardened clay. Why does the bird amass these objects? Is it impelled by a collector's instinct less perfect than that of the Bower-bird? There is no reason to suppose this. Nor does it appear that he wishes to make the nest heavier and prevent it by this ballast from being blown about by every breeze when the couple are out, and the young not heavy enough to ensure the stability of the edifice. The part played by these little balls is much more remarkable, if we may trust the evidence of the natives, as confirmed by competent European observers. Thus Mr. H. A. Severn writes :—"I have been informed on safe authority that the Indian Bottle-bird protects his nest at night by sticking several of these glow-beetles around the entrance by means of clay; and only a few days back an intimate friend of my own was watching three rats on a roof-rafter of his bungalow when a glow-fly lodged very close to them ; the rats immediately scampered off."[1] These observations are confirmed by Captain Briant, as reported by Professor R. Dubois.[2] In tropical regions luminous

[1] "Notes on the Indian Glow-fly," *Nature*, 23rd June 1881.

[2] *Science et Nature*, t. iv. (1885), No. 94, p. 232.

FIG. 43.

insects give out a brilliant light, of which the Glow-worms of northern countries can only give a feeble idea. These flying or climbing stars are the constellations of virgin forests. In South America the Indians utilise one of these insects, the *Cucujo*, by fastening it to the great toe like a little lantern, and profit by its light to find their road or to preserve

FIG. 44.

their naked feet from snakes. The first missionaries to the Antilles, lacking oil for their lamps, sometimes replaced them by Fire-flies to read matins by.[1] The *Melicourvis baya* had already discovered this method of lighting, and the mysterious little balls of clay were nothing more than candlesticks in which

[1] P. Dutertre, *Hist. des Antilles française*, 1667.

these birds set Glow-worms, when they are fresh, to act as candles. The entrance to the nest is thus luminous. (Fig. 44.) Apparently this lighting up is a defensive measure, for the birds have nothing to do at night except to sleep, and must be rather incommoded than cheered by this light. But the terrible enemy of all broods, the Snake, is, it is said, frightened by this illumination, which is able to penetrate the meshes of the nest, and will not dare to enter. The system is ingenious, and the Roman Emperors, when they used burning Christians as torches, were only plagiarising from this little bird, which paves with martyrs the threshold of its house of love.

# CHAPTER VIII.

## CONCLUSION.

DEGREE OF PERFECTION IN INDUSTRY INDEPENDENT OF ZOOLOGICAL SUPERIORITY—MENTAL FACULTIES OF THE LOWER ANIMALS OF LIKE NATURE TO MAN'S.

*Degree of perfection in industry independent of zoological superiority.*—As the result of our study we see the fundamental industries of Man dispersed throughout the animal kingdom, though not, indeed, all of them, nor the more subtle, which were only born yesterday. We may remark the extent to which intellectual manifestations of this sort are independent of the more or less elevated rank assigned to species in zoological classification. The latter, as it should be, brings together or separates beings according to their physical character. But intelligence does not depend on the whole body; its superior or inferior development is related to a certain corresponding complexity in the surface, volume, and histologic structure of the nervous centres.

It happens with the cerebral as with the other functions. An animal's superiority is not exhibited in all his organs nor in all his qualities; it results from a certain grouping of characters in which there may be weak points. The highest in organisation are not necessarily the swiftest or the strongest, any more than they are necessarily the most intelligent. It may happen; it happens in the case of Man; but it as easily fails to happen. In organisation the Horse is nearer to Man than the Ant; but it is far otherwise as regards intellectual development.

For this reason, when following the progress of any industry, I have taken my examples first in one group, then in another far-removed group, to return afterwards to the first. There are not, and cannot be, bonds between a solitary function of the being and its place in classification—a place which has been determined by the form of all the organs, without even taking into account their methods of activity.

Comparative anatomy has long since removed the barriers, once thought impassable, raised by human pride between Man and the other animals. Our bodies do not differ from theirs; and moreover, such glimpses as we are able to obtain allow us to conclude that their psychic faculties are of the same nature as our own. Man in his evolution introduces no new factor.

The industries in which the talents of animals are exercised demonstrate that, under the influence of the same environment, animals have reacted in the same manner as Man, and have formed the same combinations to protect themselves from cold or heat, to defend themselves against the attacks of enemies, and to ensure sufficient provision of food during those hard seasons of the year when the earth does not yield in abundance.

It must only be added, to avoid falling into

exaggeration, that Man excels in all the arts, of which only scattered rudiments are found among the other animals; and we may safeguard our pride by affirming that we need not fear comparison. If our intelligence is not essentially different from that of animals, we have the satisfaction of knowing that it is much superior to theirs.

# APPENDIX.

## BIBLIOGRAPHY.

*Brehm's Thierleben* is the great repository of facts concerning the social lives of the higher animals. The third edition, in ten large volumes, fully illustrated, and edited by Pechuel Lösche, has lately appeared (Leipzig und Wien, Bibliog. Institute, 1890-92). It is, indeed, as Virchow has lately termed it, "a sort of zoological library," popular in character, and almost purely descriptive. (There is a French edition of this work in nine volumes, but, with the exception of one fragment, it has not appeared in English. The nearest approach to Brehm's work in England is Cassell's *New Natural History*, and in America the *Riverside Natural History.*) It is impossible to enumerate the numberless works by travellers and others on which the knowledge of animal industries is founded. The works of Huber, Fabre, Audubon, Le Vaillant, C. St. John, Belt, Bates, Tennent, are frequently quoted in the course of this work. Many of the most important and detailed studies of animal industries are scattered through the pages of the scientific periodicals of all countries. References to a few of the chief of these studies will be found in the text.

For a scientific discussion of the phenomena of animal skill and intelligence we may perhaps best turn to Professor C. Lloyd Morgan, whose work is always both acute and cautious. In *Animal Life and Intelligence* (1890) he has furnished an excellent introduction to the subject. In his *Introduction to Comparative Psychology* (shortly to appear in the Contemporary Science Series) he discusses the fundamental problems of mental processes in animals, and the transition from animal intelligence to human intelligence. Romanes' *Mental Evolution in Animals* (1883) and other works by this writer, dealing with the same subject, but proceeding on a different method, should also be studied; and his *Animal Intelligence* (International Science Series) is an excellent critical summary of the facts. Büchner's *Aus dem Geistesleben der Thiere* (Berlin, 1877) and Houzeau's *Facultés Mentales des Animaux* (Brussels, 1877) may also be mentioned, and Espinas' *Sociétés Animales* (1877), though dealing primarily with sociology, is an original and suggestive study of great value.

As a general introduction, of a popular but not unscientific character, to all the various aspects of animal life, J. Arthur Thomson's little book, *The Study of Animal Life* (University Extension Manuals, 1892), may be recommended. At the end of Mr. Thomson's volume will be found a useful classified list of the "Best Books" on animal life.

## Gardening Ants.

The operations of various species of Gardening Ants have recently been very thoroughly investigated at Blumenau by Herr Alfred Möller, nephew of Dr. Fritz Müller ("Die Pilzgärten einiger südamerikanischer Ameisen." Heft 6 of Schimper's "Botanische Mittheilungen aus den Tropen." Jena: G. Fischer, 1893. Herr Möller's work is clearly summarised by Mr. John C. Willis in "The Fungus Gardens of certain South American Ants," *Nature*, 24th August 1893).

The ants of Blumenau chiefly differ from those described by Belt in that they form very narrow streets, in which they travel only in single file, and also that their nests occur both in the forest and in the open. The commonest species is the *Atta* (*Acromyrmex*) *discigera*, Mayr, and the workers are never more than 6.5 mm. long. There are other species of *Atta* which have very similar streets; one, the *Atta hystrix*, Latr., appears to work only at night. A minute description is given of a street of *A. discigera*, which was 26 metres long and about 1.5 cm. wide and high, roofed in in parts wherever possible. It led to a number of small Cupheas, whose leaves the ants were cutting. In the street could be seen a procession of loaded ants going towards the nest, and others empty-handed, going in the opposite direction. Some of the large workers run up and down the road unloaded, and act as road-menders if any accident happens to a part of the track. Other very small workers, which do not cut leaves, may also be seen carried upon the backs or even upon the loads of the actual leaf-cutters. An ant carrying a peculiarly shaped piece of leaf was watched from end to end of the track, and travelled the 26 m. in 70 minutes. The load was twice as heavy as itself.

The plants attacked by the ants were found to be very numerous, and the ants seemed to be very capricious in this respect, one day stripping a plant and the next day leaving it untouched.

The jaws of the ants are very strong, with serrated edges, and clash together laterally. The ant begins at the edge of a leaf, and cuts out a piece in about five minutes, revolving on one of its hind legs as a centre. When the piece is almost freed, the ant goes on to the main portion of the leaf, cuts through the last piece uniting it with the severed portion, drags up the latter, balances it on edge between its forelegs, and then, grasping it with its jaws, lifts it up above its head, so that the centre of gravity of the load is above the ant itself. It then marches off, down the stem, to the base, over the ground to the end of the street, and along this to the nest, travelling at a very uniform speed, and never letting go its load. The weight thus carried was found, on an average, to be twice that of the ant; but many were found carrying heavier loads, even as much as ten times their own weight!

The nests are usually below the surface of the soil, but covered, wherever necessary, with a thick mass of withered pieces of leaves and twigs, etc. They may be as much as 1½ metres in diameter. In the nests of all species examined there is found, filling up the interior, a curious grey spongy mass, full of chambers, like a coarse sponge, in which the ants may be seen running about, and in which, here and there, occur eggs, larvæ, and pupæ. This is the fungus garden. It is separated from the roof and lateral walls of the nest by a clear space. The walls and roof are much thicker in winter than in summer; one nest examined had a roof 25 cm. thick and wall 40 cm. The garden consists of two parts, differently coloured, but not very sharply marked off from each other. The older part is yellowish-red in colour; the newly-built portions, forming the surface of the garden, are of a blue-black colour. It is this part which is of the greater importance to the ants.

The garden is found, on examination, to consist of an immense conglomeration of small round particles of not more than .5 mm. in diameter, of a dark green colour when quite fresh, then blue-black, and finally yellowish-red. They are penetrated by, and enveloped in, white fungus hyphæ, which hold the particles together. These hyphæ are similar throughout the nest.

Strewn thickly upon the surface of the garden are seen round white bodies about .25 mm. in diameter; they always occur in the nests, except in the very young portion of the gardens. They consist of aggregations of peculiar swollen hyphæ, and are termed by Möller the "Kohl-rabi clumps." The hyphæ swell out at the ends into large spherical thickenings, filled with richly vacuolated protoplasm like the ordinary hyphæ. These clumps of "Kohl-rabi" are only found on the surface of the garden, and form the principal food of the ants; they have no doubt reached their present form under the cultivation and selection of the ants. The fungus was found to belong to the genus *Rozites*, and the species was named *R. gongylophora*. A microscopic examination of the particles of which the garden is composed shows that they contain remains of leaves; bits of epidermis, stomata, spiral vessels, etc., occur in them.

If a nest is broken into and the fungus garden scattered, the ants collect it as quickly as possible, especially the younger parts, taking as much trouble over it as over the larvæ. They also cover it up again as soon as possible to protect it from the light. A nest, 1 metre × 50 cm., was opened, and in twenty-four hours the ants had put on a new roof 10 cm. deep.

Some ants' nests were placed under a bell jar and supplied with leaves; they made no use of them and presently died. If they were supplied with a piece of "garden," they rebuilt it and covered it so far as they could. It was seen to shrink from day to day, the ants bringing out the old pieces and adding them to the wall; finally it was exhausted and the ants died. Others were starved for five days, and then supplied with a bit of garden; they at once began to eat the Kohl-rabi clumps. Finally, by supplying the ants with bits of garden, a damp sandy floor, and fresh leaves, they were induced to build in captivity. The dish in which they worked was covered by a glass lid, and when this was covered with a dark cloth or otherwise kept dark, the ants built under it without covering the garden. In this way the whole process was observed. An ant bringing in a piece of leaf proceeds to cut it into halves, repeating the process till it has got a very small piece left, which it holds between its fore feet and turns round, crushing it in its jaws until the whole is reduced to a round ball of pulp about .25 mm. thick.

This it then takes and adds to the garden. So well is the kneading performed that no single cell remains uninjured, and it was observed that the hyphæ of the fungus grew through and round one of these particles within a few hours. Belt supposed that this process was performed by the small workers above-mentioned, but it is not so, as we have just seen. The small workers perform the function of weeding the garden, and this is so well done that a portion of it removed and grown in a nutrient solution gives a perfectly pure culture, not even containing bacteria!

In the course of these investigations it was found that somewhat similar fungus gardens occur in the nests of the hairy ant, *Apterostigma*, but the fungus appeared to belong to a different genus, and the hairy ants, who live in decaying wood and have small gardens built of bits of wood-fibre, bettle-dung, etc., have not succeeded in cultivating and selecting Kohl-rabi to the same high degree. An allied genus of ants, *Cyphomyrmex*, were also found to be fungus-growers.

This elaborate study, which is illustrated by beautiful plates and photographs of the mushroom gardens, constitutes, as Mr. Willis (whose summary has here been followed) remarks, one of the most fascinating contributions to our knowledge of mycology and of animal industries which have been made for many years.

# INDEX.